Dearest Mother,

We pray that you enjoy this book of prayer readings everyday of the year. And when you do, say a little prayer for, as we'll be praying for you.

All our love,

Patty & Marvin

A TREASURY OF LIVING FAITH

Catholic Devotions For Every Day Of The Year

The Best Devotions from
Past Issues of *LIVING FAITH*
(formerly **LIVING WORDS**)

Selected and Edited by
JAMES E. ADAMS

Creative Communications for the Parish, Inc.
10300 Watson Road
St. Louis, MO 63127

Imprimatur:
Msgr. Maurice Byrne
St. Louis Archdiocese

An imprimatur is an official declaration that published material is free of doctrinal and moral error. It does not mean that officials granting the imprimatur agree with all the opinions and statements in the book.

Creative Communications for the Parish
10300 Watson Road
St. Louis, MO 63127-1187

International Standard Book Number: 0-9629585-1-4

Cover Art: 'Afternoon At Pardigon'
by **Henri Edmond Delacroix**

Illustrations: Kathye Arrington
Cover Design: James E. Adams

Printed in the United States

Editor's Preface

When Creative Communications for the Parish began publishing a quarterly magazine of Catholic devotions, we wondered how Catholics would take to brief, daily Bible-based reflections and prayers. The answer was not long in coming. After just a few years, ***LIVING FAITH*** (formerly ***LIVING WORDS***) has become one of the most widely circulated Catholic devotional magazines in the world and has become a fixture in the private devotional practice of thousands of Catholics.

One appealing feature of ***LIVING FAITH*** is, I believe, the rhythm of **daily** reflection. There are many artificial ways in which time is measured. But the day, that short, natural block of time marked by the coming and going of the sun, remains the most basic unit in our lives. Dietrich Bonhoeffer, the German pastor and theologian executed by the Nazis, spoke these wise words on the religious significance of the daily rhythm:

> Each morning is a new beginning of our life. Each day is a finished whole. The present day marks the boundary of our cares and concerns. (Mt. 6:34, Jas. 4:14) It is long enough to find God or to lose God, to keep faith or fall into disgrace. God created day and night for us so we need not wander without boundaries, but may be able to see every morning the goal of the evening ahead. Just as the ancient sun rises anew every day, so the eternal mercy of God is new every morning.

This ***Treasury***, the second such volume we have published, consists of a year's worth of the best of previous devotions from ***LIVING FAITH*** (and ***LIVING WORDS***). Each devotion begins with a passage from Sacred Scripture that provides a basic theme. A brief reflection follows, either taken from a published work of an outstanding Catholic author and leader, or from our own writers, who include priests, sisters and laity. Many devotions end with a one-sentence prayer.

Besides varied themes about all aspects of prayer, readers of this ***Treasury*** will frequently find herein such themes as the need to recognize God's infinite and abiding love for us, the need for trust in God and the need to submit to God's will. Other frequent themes include the importance of gratitude, generosity, gentleness, compassion, humility and joy in the life of Christians.

We hope that all ***Treasury*** readers will be inspired and encouraged by these devotions, and that their Catholic faith will be enriched each day by what they read here. But we also hope readers will be inspired to do additional spiritual reading—especially more reading of the Bible.

My thanks to three groups that have made this book possible. First, to the general and Catholic publishing firms that year after year provide good spiritual books (some of which are quoted in this ***Treasury***). Second, my thanks to our team of ***LIVING FAITH*** writers who have contributed many spiritual insights over the past years. Third, my special thanks to our many loyal ***LIVING FAITH*** readers and supporters. May you—and all who use this book—be blessed by it.

James E. Adams

The Love Of God

■ **As proof that you are children, God sent the spirit of his Son into our hearts, crying out, "Abba, Father!"**
Galatians 4:6

God loves us as our Father. The parable of the prodigal son expresses this truth most vividly. You recall that moment when the son came to his senses, decided to return home and set off for his father's house. "While he was still a long way off, his father caught sight of him and was deeply moved. He ran out to meet him, threw his arms around his neck and kissed him." (Luke 15:20) This is the fatherly love of God, a love always ready to forgive, eager to welcome us back . . . The reality of God's love for us as our father is why Jesus told us to say, "Abba, Father."

God loves us as a Mother also. God asks, through the Prophet Isaiah, "Can a mother forget her infant, be without tenderness for the child of her womb? Even should she forget, I will never forget you." (Isaiah 49:15) God's love is tender and merciful, patient, full of understanding. The love of God is indeed depicted and has been experienced as the compassionate love of a mother.

Pope John Paul II
Sermon in San Francisco, 9/17/'87

O God, help me realize more fully each day of this new year what it means to be your child.

A Little Love

■ **Little children, let us love in deed and in truth, and not merely talk about it.** 1 John 3:18

Love does not live on words, nor can it be explained by words—especially that love which serves God, which comes from God and which finds God and touches God. We must reach the heart, and to reach the heart as we must, love is proved in deeds. . .

Perhaps it is only a smile, a little visit, or simply the fact of building a fire for someone, writing a letter for a blind person, bringing a few lumps of coal, finding a pair of shoes, reading for someone. This is only a little bit, yes, a very tiny bit, but it will be our love of God in action . . .

Never think that a small action done to your neighbor is not worth much. It is not how much we do that is pleasing to God, but how much love we put into the doing. That is what the good God looks for—because God is love and God made us in the divine image to love and to be loved.

Mother Teresa
Love: A Fruit Always in Season

Jesus, soften my heart so that I may begin to love others in deed and not just in theory.

Manual For Christians

■ **Follow me.** John 1:43

Here is a simple two-word set of instructions for realizing eternal life: "Follow me."

"Follow me." Pray as I prayed, for guidance, for strength, for wisdom and for a love that would endure.

"Follow me." Love others as I loved Mary, Lazarus, Zacchaeus, the Samaritan Woman, even Pilate, Herod and those who didn't understand.

"Follow me." Suffer when the central commitment of life calls for witnessing to the Truth even to death.

"Follow me." Reach out to the poor, the depressed, the victims of injustice, the lonely.

"Follow me." Forgive those who cause hurt and harm, whose hunger for love is twisted and perverted.

"Follow me." In faith, hope and love until we sit together at the banquet table of our Father.

Joan Weber Laflamme

Jesus, give me the faith and the courage to follow you this day.

Soul-Searching Question

■ **When Jesus turned around and noticed them following him, he asked them, "What are you looking for?"** John 1:38

I imagine myself following behind Jesus. He turns, peers at me and asks me, **"What are you looking for?"**

Jesus, I am not always sure what I am looking for. I think I am looking for happiness, not the kind that comes from success, but rather that joy of the spirit, that deep sense of being utterly at home, utterly at peace in my soul, in harmony with all of creation and with God the Creator. Jesus, I guess I am looking for my real home. Can you help me find that home?

Jesus, I think I am looking also for myself, the real me rather than the disjointed, harried and makeshift self that I have built up in order to try to get by in this world. I don't know who I am, but I know that this phony self that daily passes for me is not the full and real me.

Jesus, can you help me find myself?

James E. Adams

Finding God

■ **Then you shall be radiant at what you see, your heart shall throb and overflow.** Isaiah 60:5

I feel I must give the lie to anyone who says, "I'm looking for God, but I can't find God!" Let that person try to do everything in the truth, free from the demon of pride and the suffocating density of egoism. Let every trace of racism be rooted out, let everyone be welcomed as a brother or sister, and . . . you will see, you will see!

Live love. Act truth. Honor life. And it will be the God beyond you whom you live, act and honor. God will not come to you because you have become "good." God was already there. God has always been coming and always is coming. But now you see God because you have purified your eyes, softened your heart and stooped down.

Remember, God was already there . . . the only difficulty was that you were unable to see. Now you identify love and light and life more and more with God. You see God even if God is still veiled and expressed in the mysterious parable of created things.

Carlo Carretto
The God Who Comes

Dear God, help me to see divine goodness in all that surrounds me this day.

Unconditional Love

■ **I have written this to make you realize that you possess eternal life.** 1 John 5:13

The love of God is so great that it goes beyond the limits of human language, beyond the grasp of artistic expression, beyond human understanding. And yet, it is concretely embodied in God's son, Jesus Christ, and in his Body, the Church. Once again today, here in this place, I repeat to all of you the ageless proclamation of the Gospel: **God loves you!**

God loves you all, without distinction, without limit. God loves those of you who are elderly, who feel the burden of old age. God loves those of you who are sick, those who are suffering from AIDS. God loves the relatives and friends of the sick and those who care for them. The Creator loves us all with an unconditional and everlasting love. . .

I urge you all to open your hearts to God's love, to respond by your prayers and by the deeds of your lives. Let go of your doubts and fears, and let the mercy of God draw you to the divine heart. Open the doors of your hearts to our God, who is rich in mercy.

Pope John Paul II
Sermon in San Francisco, 9/17'87

Dear God, may I learn more deeply today the richness of your love for me.

The Gift Of Divine Life

■ **Whoever acknowledges that Jesus is the Son of God, God remains in him and he in God.** 1 John 4:15

Christianity is what the living God does in relation to us, what the living God of grace gives us—in forgiveness, redemption, justification, and the communications of his own glory. Since, however, what God gives is not, in the last resort, a created gift, but himself, Christianity is ultimately simply the eternal God himself, coming to a human being and influencing this person by his grace, so that the person freely opens his or her heart for the whole glorious infinite life of the triune God to enter the poor heart of this tiny creature.

Fr. Karl Rahner, S.J.
Words of Faith

Most Favored Status

■ **This is my beloved Son. My favor rests on him.**
Matthew 3:17

We who are the followers of Jesus must always be open to the possibility that this "voice from heaven" may want to include us. Look up into the skies and hear the truth: "You are my beloved; my favor rests on you."

At our baptism we were anointed with the Holy Spirit and with power. As refreshing as these waters of baptism were we know enough about the Paschal Mystery to be aware that these waters have also been waters of bitterness.

To be a beloved one favored by God does not mean all sweetness and light. To go down into the waters with Christ is to enter into a life-giving death.

Pray for the courage to accept all the faces of your baptism.

Sr. Macrina Wiederkehr, O.S.B.

'This Too Will Pass'

■ **There is a season for everything.** Ecclesiastes 3:1

A great Eastern monarch once asked a wise man the secret of serenity. "Whatever happens, I say, 'this, too, will pass away'," said the wise man. Earlier translations of Scripture used a similar expression, "it came to pass," which connoted that whatever was happening, pain or happiness, was not there to stay but would pass on.

When joy comes into our lives, it is a gift from God to enrich us, to strengthen us—and then pass on. We interfere with its purpose when we cling to it and try to force it to remain. Only if we let it go when its time is up will we know the peace that comes from acceptance and gratitude. Likewise with sorrow. The awareness that it will pass gives us courage. It also helps us realize that each cross that Christ allows in our lives has a purpose. Once that purpose has been fulfilled, the pain will move on. Even the ultimate sorrow of death is meant to give way to a glorious resurrection.

Sr. Mary Terese Donze, A.S.C.

O God, help me to know when to release my joys and sorrows into your hands.

Moved With Pity

■ Moved with pity, he stretched out his hand, touched him, and said to him, "I do will it. Be made clean."
Mark 1:41

Many saints remind us that Jesus has no hands but ours, no heart but ours, to bring his presence into the world here and now. Jesus calls us to be "moved with pity" for one another, to "stretch out" our hands to one another, and touch one another, that we might be healed.

Among today's lepers are the man or woman with AIDS, that wild-looking homeless woman on the street, those suffering from drug addiction, the battered wife, the abused child. We tend to avoid such people "like leprosy," unless, of course, we allow ourselves to be "moved with pity."

But what about closer to home? How often do we see smaller or more hidden afflictions in those who people our daily lives and respond superficially or with indifference? Our spouse, our children, our neighbors, our co-workers, all bear burdens of many sizes and shapes, and they deserve our compassion, kindness, patience and encouragement. Sometimes we must make a conscious effort and say, " I do will it."

Mitch Finley

Jesus, when others need me, may I be moved with pity and stirred into action.

Joys Of Being A Pilgrim

■ **By acknowledging themselves to be strangers and foreigners on the earth, they showed that they were seeking a homeland.** Hebrews 11:13-14

Being a pilgrim is not all that bad when you consider the alternatives. It certainly beats traveling with no special place to go. And it has it all over being stuck someplace unpleasant. Indeed, one of the joys of living here on earth in Christian faith is remembering that we are pilgrims and not just wandering travelers.

There is a big difference. As pilgrims we know where we are going and that it is a good place. We need not worry about how we are going because we know with whom we are going. All we need say is, "I would like to go along!" The Lord takes care of the rest. . . Thus I am satisfied to sit back and watch the busy comings and goings of this life. I am not quite sure where I came from. I do not have a clear idea of where I am going. But that is the Lord's business. He is here and he will take me with him in good time. In the meantime I can sit and listen to what he has to say to me here—stories about how it will be at home with him, further instructions about how to get there. I am confident with the confidence of a pilgrim.

Fr. Donald X. Burt
The Inn of the Samaritan

Divine Initiative

■ **Beloved, we, for our part, love God, because he first loved us.** 1 John 4:19

St. John certainly put things in perspective. My focus is ordinarily on what I'm doing or not doing to get closer to God, how I'm trying to live as a disciple of Jesus or what my spiritual life is like. It is as though I had one day, out of the blue, just decided on my own to point my life in this particular direction. But nothing could be further from the truth.

God is the beginning and the source; we can choose to respond to Love Eternal or to resist, but that is all. It is a humbling realization, but one that can set us free: because God is in charge, we need never worry about generating our own happiness, love or meaning in life. Instead, we can try to school ourselves to accept in faith and gratitude that which is constantly being given us.

Easier said than done, perhaps, but even our impulse to try will come, not from some inner resource we have, but from God's great bounty.

Mark Neilsen

O God, may I always be grateful for the good things that come to me from your love.

Freeing Others

■ **"Untie him," Jesus said, "and let him go free."**
John 11:44

The account of Lazarus restored to life is so rich that we often overlook the detail of the unbinding of Lazarus by his friends. Surely the force of restored life could have itself loosed Lazarus. But God wanted the mourners to know how fully they shared in giving Lazarus—and each other—the gift of life.

Our life-energy increases in proportion to the love with which we reach out to others, and our compassion prepares the way for hope in others' hearts. When discouragement and fear have entombed me, the caring presence of friends has persuaded me to move out of myself again.

May the awareness of our own limitations help us to recognize and to reach out to those seeking freedom and the fullness of life.

Sr. Audrey Synnott

Jesus, may I always be ready and willing to untie others and do my part to set them free.

Pour Out Your Heart

Pour out your hearts before God, our refuge.
Psalm 62:9

God, our loving Father, says to us: You do not have to be clever to please me; all you have to do is want to love me. Just speak to me as you would to anyone of whom you are very fond.

Are there any people you want to pray for? Say their names to me, and ask of me as much as you like. I am generous, and know all their needs, but I want you to show your love for them and me by trusting me to do what I know is best.

Is there anything you want for your soul? If you like, you can write out a long list of all your needs, and read it to me. Tell me of the things you feel guilty about. I will forgive you if you will accept it. Just tell me about your pride, your touchiness, self-centeredness, meanness and laziness. I still love you in spite of these. Do not be ashamed. There are many saints in heaven who had the same faults, but they prayed to me, and little by little, their faults were corrected.

Do not hesitate to ask me for blessings for the body and mind . . . I can give everything, and I always do give everything needed to make souls holier for those who truly want it.

Fr. John Catoir
Enjoy the Lord

January 15

A Bible Lesson

■ **Many of his followers said, "This is intolerable language. How could anyone accept it?"** John 6:60

The biblical message may be disconcerting, ambiguous, even frightening. It may shock our reason into unbelief, and we many have to struggle with it as a scandal. Indeed, when closely examined, the Bible may pose a threat to what has hitherto seemed to us to be "faith."

There is nothing comfortable about the Bible—until we manage to get so used to it that we make it comfortable for ourselves. But then we are perhaps too used to it and too at home in it. Let us not be too sure we know the Bible just because we have learned not to be astonished at it, just because we have learned not to have problems with it. Have we perhaps learned at the same time not to really pay attention to it? Have we ceased to question the Bible and be questioned by it? Have we ceased to fight it? Perhaps our reading is no longer serious.

For most people, the understanding of the Bible is, and should be, a struggle.

Thomas Merton
Opening the Bible

O God, teach me to live by your word—especially when that word seems so difficult!

The Pure Of Heart

■ **Only one day in your courts is worth more than a thousand elsewhere.** Psalm 84:11

Do we pray much too casually? One ancient mystic tells us that we should pray as though we would die at the end of the prayer. Can you imagine how pure our prayer would be if we stood in the courts of God with such incredible belief in the Divine Presence—not knowing whether we would live or die!

Yes, we approach God far too casually. We do not come to prayer expecting to be changed, expecting to be healed and renewed. Perhaps that is the reason we are so often unhappy with the results of our prayer. Perhaps God sees our unexpectant hearts and knows that we aren't expecting to be changed. God doesn't ordinarily answer our prayers *without us.* He respects our freedom and waits for us to connect with our pure hearts. That pure heart is within us, waiting, longing. Some day we will connect with that pure heart and let God transform us.

Blessed the pure-hearted; they shall see God!

Sr. Macrina Wiederkehr, O.S.B.

Dear God, may I stand before you in prayer expecting to be changed and to be healed.

Other-Worldliness

■ **Our desire is that each of you show the same zeal till the end, fully assured of that for which you hope.**

Hebrews 6:11

Hope is one of the theological virtues. This means that a continual looking forward to the eternal world is not (as some people think) a form of escapism or wishful thinking, but one of the things a Christian is meant to do. It does not mean that we are to leave the present world as it is. If you read history you will find that the Christians who did most for the present world were just those who thought most of the next. The Apostles themselves, who set in motion the conversion of the Roman Empire, the great men who built up the Middle Ages, the English Evangelicals who abolished the Slave Trade, all left their mark on Earth, precisely because their minds were occupied with Heaven. It is since Christians have largely ceased to think of the other world that they have become so ineffective in this. Aim at Heaven and you will get Earth "thrown in." Aim at Earth and you will get neither.

C.S. Lewis
The Joyful Christian

O God, restore in me a healthy interest in both heaven and earth.

The Little Things

■ **Well done, good servant! You have been faithful in this very small matter . . .** Luke 19:17

There is a kind of hidden miserliness in human nature that prevents me from employing myself fully in any event, that counts the cost of everything and wants me to save my energies for future emergencies, that fails to realize that the only way to reinforce the powers of the soul is to use them in full. Everything matters. Everything I do is important, because it is me. There is no small event in life, no negligible occasion, no minor opportunity. Everything that happens to me requires the whole of me, and by holding back and letting only half of me into the fray I only do harm to myself and stunt my growth. Lack of generosity with life is the reason I do not allow myself to develop as I know I could.

Fr. Carlos G. Valles, S.J.
Courage To Be Myself

Jesus, I am often so stingy with myself! Help me commit myself more fully and freely.

Beware Triumphalism

■ **They carried to him all those afflicted with pain; the possessed, the lunatics, the paralyzed. He cured them all.** Matthew 4:24

The true Church is the Church of the defeated, of the weak, of the poor, of those on the fringe of society.

It is a pity that the great gatherings of Christians too often take place in St. Peter's Square. It was designed by Bernini, who was the son of a pagan period that was sick with triumphalism. He designed everything as a triumph.

We must beware! In St. Peter's Square there are many lusty people to shout hosannas! But there is no sign of the Church's agony, of human agony—and everything can go wrong if we forget reality, even when everything seems fine.

Rallies of Christians are more suitable in hospitals, in prisons, in shanty towns, in mental homes, where people cry, where people suffer, where the devastation of sin is being physically endured, sin in the form of the arrogance of the rich and the powerful.

Carlo Carretto
Blessed Are You Who Believed

Jesus, when we are tempted to self-righteous arrogance, teach us humility.

Pray From The Heart

■ **For you have not spoken rightly concerning me, as has my servant Job.** Job 42:8

Any theology in which we pretend to justify God by reason is bound to be bad theology. You cannot do it. It is the theology of Job's friends. The Book of Job tells us a great deal about prayer. It says that here is a man who undergoes great evil and here are four people who come along and explain the evil logically and they tell Job why he is wrong and why he has to suffer. We talk about the patience of Job, but Job is not patient at all. In fact, he is mad at God and he is arguing with God and he is protesting against God and saying you are not right, you are wrong, you shouldn't be doing this to me. And what happens at the end of it is that God comes along and says Job is right.

The real theological message is . . . that our relations with God are person-to-person relationships, and that we don't deal with God according to some system. You don't look up in a book asking yourself, "How do I talk to God about this?" . . . The Bible says that if you really tell God what is in your heart you are doing right.

Thomas Merton
Thomas Merton in Alaska

O Holy Spirit, free me so that I may pray to the Father from the depths of my soul.

No Heart Too Hard

■ **As the Holy Spirit says, "Today, if you should hear his voice, harden not your hearts . . ."** Hebrews 3:7-8

There is no one who cannot discover and find a place in God's love. From it flows our Christian hope. There exists no one so bad, so brought down, so broken down, that he cannot find a place in that love, the love of the Father who feeds all of us, the love of the Son sacrificed for us, the love of the Spirit who enlightens us. There is no one who cannot find a place in that love. It is the source of our Christian hope.

But when someone, even someone who cannot comprehend it, receives that love, he receives it because love wants him to receive it. First and foremost, when someone receives this love there must at once be born in him some need to respond. No one can receive this love unresponsively. God does not ask that we match this love, but that we receive it humbly. Yet God wants us to try to reply to this love, to try to respond to the utmost of our human ability.

Pope John Paul II
The Light of Christ

Dear God, forgive me for the many times I have failed to respond to your infinite love.

A Prayer Of Listening

■ **Speak, Lord, for your servant is listening.**

1 Samuel 3:10

Here I am, God, struggling to hear your voice among the many voices which tug, beckon and entice. Here I am, straining to hear your whisper among the many whispers which break through my dreams and reveries, cajoling me with their subtlety. Here I am, searching the stillness for signs of your presence and of your will for me.

I am ready, God. Speak, I am listening. Let me know what it is you want for me. Let me hear your word, deep in my heart. Give me the clarity to see and feel and understand all that will help me respond. In the fullness of your love, teach me your wisdom so my will and your will may be one.

Remind me that it is in following you that I will discover my true happiness. Melt my resistance, God. Let me respond to your call. Let my whole being resound with "Yes" to all that you want for me.

Elizabeth-Anne Vanek

Christian Tension

■ **From the cup I drink of, you shall drink.**
Matthew 20:23

Someone said, "I have a problem. Nothing seems simple. I don't know whether it is better to do this or that. The truth is, I'm always in tension." But a wise person said, "Yes, that sounds so very typically human. So where is the problem?"

Jesus said we must take up our cross and follow him, drink from the cup he drank from. We tend to think of obvious physical or mental suffering. But we fulfill in part the call to bear the cross by simply enduring the tensions of our daily lives just as Jesus did. He needed to remain at the Temple, but that caused grief to his parents who feared he was lost. Mary noticed that the couple at Cana needed wine, but that created a rub because Jesus felt the time for miracles hadn't arrived yet. A man needed healing, but that presented a dilemma because it was the Sabbath.

Jesus' life was marked with tension. If we follow him to the Father, we also can expect that cross as well. Our goal should not be to live without tensions but to live graciously with them.

Joan Weber Laflamme

O Lord, help me each moment of this day to accept the inevitable tensions and strains.

For Love Of Money

■ **Buyers should conduct themselves as though they owned nothing, and those who make use of the world as though they were not using it, for the world as we know it is passing away.** 1 Corinthians 7:30-31

Those who love God are not much in love with money. I didn't venture to say that they don't love money at all, but rather don't love it much, as if money were to be loved, but not in a great degree. Oh, were we loving God worthily, we should have no love at all for money! Money then will be your means of pilgrimage, not the stimulant of lust; something to use for necessity, not to joy over as a means of delight.

Love God . . . use the world, but don't let the world hold you captive. You are passing on the journey you have begun; you have come here to depart, not to abide. You are passing on your journey, and this life is but a wayside inn. Use money as the traveller at an inn uses table, cup, pitcher and bed, with the purpose not of remaining, but of leaving them behind. If such you would be, you will attain to God's promises.

St. Augustine
An Augustine Treasury

O God, help me to be ever mindful that I have here no lasting home.

Stand Up And Be Counted

■ **This man is an instrument I have chosen to bring my name to the Gentiles.** Acts 9:15

We all have to realize that the call to bring Jesus to the world is not a call to walk on water. But it is a call to stand up and be counted. Remember the haunting question: If you were being arrested for being a Christian, would there be enough evidence to convict you? The Jesus who asks to be recognizable in me isn't perfect. I could never manage that. Rather it is the Jesus who labors in me, who consoles me and supports me in my human weakness, that must shine out of me. It is the Jesus who said to Paul, "My strength will work through your weakness."

All of us carry the treasure of this loving Jesus in fragile vessels of clay. We cannot be expected to exhibit perfection, but we must be willing to stand up and to offer our personal testimonials to grace. You and I should want to say to the world, as Paul did after his conversion, "Jesus has touched my life. By his kindness, by his encouragement and by his challenge, Jesus has made all the difference in my life. I was blind and now I see. I was lost and now I'm found!" Yet I always add: "Please be patient. God is not finished with me."

Fr. John Powell, S.J.
Through Seasons of the Heart

True Happiness

■ **To Timothy, my child whom I love . . . I yearn to see you again. That would make my happiness complete.**
2 Timothy 1:2, 4

A happiness that is sought for ourselves alone can never be found, for a happiness that is diminished by being shared is not big enough to make us happy.

There is a false and momentary happiness in self-satisfaction, but it always leads to sorrow because it narrows and deadens our spirit. True happiness is found in unselfish love, a love which increases in proportion as it is shared. There is no end to the sharing of love, and, therefore, the potential happiness of such love is without limit. Infinite sharing is the law of God's inner life. He has made the sharing of ourselves the law of our own being, so that it is in loving others that we best love ourselves. In disinterested activity we best fulfill our own capacities to act and to be.

Yet there can never be happiness in compulsion. It is not enough for love to be shared. It must be shared freely. That is to say it must be given, not merely taken.

Thomas Merton
No Man Is An Island

Jesus, help me to learn sharing, which is the secret of true happiness.

Lowering The Pressure

■ **Let us be concerned for each other.** Hebrews 10:24

One night when St. John Bosco was still a small boy, he dreamed he was surrounded by a pack of wild beasts. He was trying to bring them under control by violence. Suddenly, a beautiful woman stood before him. "Go gently," she told him. He ceased his violence, and the beasts little by little changed into lambs that followed wherever he led.

Our desire to change others may not be taking the form of physical violence, but so long as we are trying to use any type of pressure on our family, our friends— even ourselves—to force change, we are exercising a form of violence. We are setting up a standard and expecting them or ourselves to measure up to it.

Concern for others will be genuine only when it takes the form of an affirming support that allows those we wish to help the freedom to develop their potential for good—and to do it at their own pace.

Sr. Mary Terese Donze, A.S.C.

O Gentle One, help me to be firm but always gentle in my dealings with others.

God's Surprises

Jesus said to them, "Come after me, and I will make you fishers of men." And at once they left their nets and followed him. Mark 1:17-18

Peter and Andrew, followed by John and James, left everything they knew—family and work—to follow Jesus. And they did it "at once," no hesitation. This wasn't the Jesus whose miracles had spread his fame. It was Jesus at the beginning of his ministry. The Transfiguration comes later. Yet Jesus touched them and they dropped all things to follow him.

How willing are we to drop what we are doing to follow Jesus? This need not be a dramatic change of vocation, though for some it might be. There are moments of major decisions many times in our lives. We are to pray for insight into God's will, read the Scriptures, discuss with others how best to follow Jesus in this moment.

But each day, God sends us little surprises—people not in our appointment book, unscheduled problems with our children. These calls to alter our own agendas are generally opportunities to embrace what God has in mind for us. The more faithful we can be in these little decisions, the more likely we are to be faithful in the bigger ones.

James McGinnis

The Ways Of Love

■ **When you are behaving as if you loved someone, you will shortly come, in fact, to love that person.** *C. S. Lewis*

Love is patient; love is kind. Love is not jealous, it does not put on airs, it is not snobbish. Love is never rude, it is not self-seeking, it is not prone to anger; neither does it brood over injuries. Love does not rejoice in what is wrong but rejoices with the truth. There is no limit to love's forbearance, to its trust, its power to endure.

Love never fails. Prophecies will cease, tongues will be silent, knowledge will pass away. Our knowledge is imperfect and our prophesying is imperfect. When the perfect comes, the imperfect will pass away. When I was a child, I used to talk like a child, think like a child, reason like a child. When I became a man, I put childish ways aside. Now we see indistinctly, as in a mirror; then we shall see face to face. My knowledge is imperfect now; then I shall know even as I am known. There are in the end three things that last; faith, hope and love, and the greatest of these is love.

1 Corinthians 13:4-13

The Friends Of God

■ **Harken to my words, O Lord, attend to my sighing. Heed my call for help, my king and my God! To you I pray, O Lord.** Psalm 5:2-3

Often prayer consoles us, but not always.

We frequently hear of the saints spending a whole night in prayer. Perhaps many of these prayers were serene, but I suspect that often God heard some angry prayers that the saints were reluctant to express while other people were around.

The story is told, for example, that St. Teresa of Avila (the 16th Century Spanish contemplative and reformer of the Carmelite Order) was once crossing a river by oxcart. When the cart tipped over, Teresa was drenched. She promptly prayed: *"God, if that's the way you treat your friends, it's no wonder you have so few of them."* Many nights of anxious prayer about other matters may well have been summarized in that one-liner.

Fr. Pat McCloskey
When You Are Angry With God

Lord, every now and again please send me a blessing with no disguise!

'Spoiling The Poor'

■ **Blest are you poor; the reign of God is yours.**
Luke 6:20

As I read the Gospel, I cannot but smile at those who tell us that we are spoiling the poor in offering them our free service. I think no one has given us more than God has, who has given us everything freely. And it is not so bad to have at least one religious order that spoils the poor, when everybody else spoils the rich.

I am deeply impressed by the fact that before explaining the word of God, before presenting to the crowds the eight beatitudes, Jesus had compassion and gave them food. Only then did he begin to teach.

What Our Lady does is similar; at the moment Jesus entered her life, at the very moment when—so to speak—she made her first communion, Mary hurried to go and serve Elizabeth. And what did she do? She became the handmaiden of the Lord.

We too—you and I—have to begin by giving Jesus to others. People nowadays suffer much, but above all they are hungry for God.

Mother Teresa
Heart of Joy

O God, help us to recognize hunger and poverty—and to do our part to alleviate them.

God's Vulnerability

■ **Because he himself was tested through what he suffered, he is able to help those who are being tested.**

Hebrews 2:18

The way of God is the way of weakness. The great news of the Gospel is precisely that God became small and vulnerable, and hence bore fruit among us. The most fruitful life ever lived is the life of Jesus, who did not cling to his divine power but became as we are. Jesus brought us new life in ultimate vulnerability. It is in this extreme vulnerability that our salvation was won. The fruit of this poor and failing existence is eternal life for all who believe in him.

It is very hard for us to grasp even a little bit of the mystery of God's vulnerability. Yet, when we have eyes to see and ears to hear we can see it in many ways and many places. We can see it when a child is born, the fruit of the love of two people who came together without defenses and embraced in weakness. We can see it in the grateful smiles of poor people and in the warm affection of the handicapped. We can see it every time people ask forgiveness and are reconciled.

Fr. Henri J. M. Nouwen
Lifesigns

When I want to control everything, help me, Jesus, to recall your powerlessness.

Mystery Of Helplessness

■ **This child is destined to be the downfall and the rise of many in Israel, a sign that will be opposed.**

Luke 2:34

God enters the temple not as a potentate or mighty one but as a small child in his mother's arms. The king of glory does not arrive in a great demonstration of human strength and power, not with great pomp and noise. He does not enter causing terror or destruction. He enters the temple as he entered the world, as an infant. He enters in silence, in poverty, and in the company of the poor and the wise.

God comes as a little child—God, the creator of all, the omnipotent Lord of heaven and earth, the king of glory. God's first entrance into the temple of his people is wrapped in the mystery of helplessness. Yes, his power is concealed in simplicity and in the defenselessness of a babe . . .

Simeon predicted that Jesus would be a "sign that will be opposed." These words reveal the whole messianic way of Christ from his birth to his death on the cross. Jesus is destined to be for all ages a sign of rejection . . . of contradiction.

Pope John Paul II
Draw Near to God

Jesus, help me to accept the mystery of helplessness that is revealed in your incarnation.

This Wonder-ful World

■ Give thanks to the Lord of lords, for his mercy endures forever; Who alone does great wonders . . .

Psalm 136:3-4

When I was younger and more impatient I used to get bored when the junior scouts opened their tents and gazed curiously and affectionately at the woods and at the tiny animals under the yellowing leaves. It seemed a waste of time. I would have preferred to have taught catechism in some church.

I was immature and did not understand that the best catechism is to fix our eyes on created things because through things God begins to speak to us. It may be, through teaching catechism to bored students sitting on benches, teaching abbreviated formulas and intellectual summaries, that we have destroyed all, leaving them sad and absent before the mystery of God.

Today, how I should like to replace a catechism lesson with a walk in the fields, offering to a boy who lives buried in the inhuman cemetery of the city, the wonderful discovery of a sparrow's nest. For is not wonder the first, unconscious meeting with mystery? Does not wonder give birth to the first prayer? Does not the power to contemplate involve first the power to be awed?

Carlo Carretto
The God Who Comes

Apostolic Ministry

■ **They expelled many demons, anointed the sick with oil, and worked many cures.** Mark 6:13

How magnificently the life-giving power of the Spirit revealed itself in the ministry of the Apostles! The radiance of their faith and the genuine warmth of their compassion were lightning rods that "grounded" the grace of God so that it satisfied the needs of God's people and encouraged the growth of the Apostles' faith as well.

How strongly, I ask myself, do I believe that the Spirit lives as vibrantly in me today? Do I act as if I knew Jesus was ministering through my touch, my speech, my service of others? No less than Peter or Paul, my listening, loving presence to another person in a time of grief or trial calls down an anointing of peace and fortitude on both of us. In fact, as I listen to how a person has struggled with a difficulty, some aspect of their experience usually gives me an insight about how to live with a loss or hardship of my own.

May each of us be graced with the daily awareness of God-with-us, and may that assurance fill us with joy and courage as the reign of God becomes more evident in and through our presence to others.

Sr. Audrey Synnott, R.S.M.

Hearing God's Call

■ **"Here I am," I said. "Send me!"** Isaiah 6:8

There is a child-like simplicity to Isaiah's "Here I am," a spontaneity and openness which we rarely associate with adults. There is no hesitation, no weighing of costs, but simply a willingness to serve. For Isaiah, God's call is enough.

Responding to God with complete trust does not come easily. Unless we walk closely with God, we may not even be aware of being called to anything more than our usual routines. We drown out God's voice with our own agendas. And if we do hear a call, we can only respond generously if we have learned to give and trust over a period of time. How we respond, then, depends on how much attention we have paid to God's presence in our lives.

Isaiah was a man of vision who walked closely with God. His writings reveal an intimate relationship with the God of whom he speaks with tenderness and compassion. Little wonder that he heard the call to prophecy so distinctly or that he answered eagerly.

Elizabeth-Anne Vanek

O God, give me an ear eager to hear when you call and a heart ready and willing to respond.

Our Loving God

■ As the heavens are high above the earth, so surpassing is his kindness to those who fear him.

Psalm 103:11

We are very accustomed to being loved conditionally. Parents love us if we are obedient. Teachers love us if we do well in school. Friends of the opposite sex love us if we look or dress the right way.

But with God there are no "ifs." God loves us unconditionally, "warts and all." He is infinite in patience and compassion.

Not that this should lull us into complacency. To develop our awareness of God's love is not some pleasant invitation we can accept or refuse at will—it is our responsibility: for only when we have truly known God's love can we be channels through which he can touch our sisters and brothers. God does not work by magic; he works through people. God's love is our consolation, but it must also be our challenge.

Nancy Benvenga

Jesus, I accept the challenge of loving others; help me to meet that challenge today.

'The Hole In The Soul'

■ **Wicked designs come from the deep recesses of the heart: acts of fornication, theft, murder, adulterous conduct, greed, maliciousness, deceit, sensuality, envy, blasphemy, arrogance, and obtuse spirit.**

Mark 7:22-23

Until you recognize, love and embrace your poverty, you will never hear the Gospel. . .

You must break through to your own poverty, your own limitations, your own powerlessness. . . I call it the hole in the soul. Until we discover that hole in the soul, that place where we are radically broken, where we cannot do what we want to do, where we are powerless, we will not break through to a Gospel spirituality. . . **there is no other way to come to wisdom except through the hole in the soul. . .**

We cannot stuff the part of ourselves that we hate, fear or deny. Nothing gets stuffed. . .it just comes back in a different form. (That is why in confession) the important thing is to name the reality, to own it, to taste it. What's going on here? What is the trap I am hopelessly caught in?

Fr. Richard Rohr, O.F.M.
from *Breathing Under Water*

Holy Spirit, reveal to me my poverty—and help me to own it!

God's Infinite Mercy

■ **His mercy is from age to age on those who fear him.**
Luke 1:50

All we can do is flee to God and his mercy. Poor, helpless, frail creatures, we can only beg him to make the crooked straight, to bring low the mountains, to make the darkness light.

God stands by us, even if we cannot always be said to have stood by him. He loves us, even if we are sometimes strangely forgetful of him in our daily lives, even if our hearts seem to be more attached to many things than to him, the God of our hearts and our portion forever. He is the one who is faithful to us, good to us, close to us, merciful to us. He is our light. He has come and always longs to come to us more abundantly. We should be optimistic about God and his mercy, for we have no right to entertain a low view of God and his mercy. We do not judge ourselves. If instead we let him judge, being patient with him and with ourselves, faithful to him, accepting the life he himself accepted when he assumed our humanity, trusting in him, then his judgment when our day comes will be grace and peace from God.

Fr. Karl Rahner, S.J.
Words of Faith

Lord, when I am tempted to give up on myself, help me to remember your infinite love.

Gathering The Crumbs

■ **"Please, Lord," she replied, "even the dogs under the table eat the family's leavings."** Mark 7:28

I am in awe of this woman's persistence, humility and vision. She simply wouldn't take no for an answer. Put-downs didn't seem to faze her. And why was that? It was because her heart was undivided. She knew what she wanted. She had come to Jesus seeking help for someone she loved. She would not allow her own hurt feelings to stand in the way of her prayer for help. She believed he was Lord! He called her a dog and she reminded him that the dogs get the crumbs that fall from the table . . .

I am touched by her vision that recognizes nourishment even in the crumbs. Crumbs are little things, a little portion of something much larger. Crumbs are insignificant. Crumbs are what most people overlook, even in the spiritual life, because they are so busy grabbing for the whole loaf. But this woman didn't overlook them. Her heart was too single and pure to miss even the opportunity of a crumb.

Sr. Macrina Wiederkehr, O.S.B.
A Tree Full of Angels

O God, help me to recognize the spiritual nourishment in the "crumbs" of everyday life.

On Guard

■ **Create a pure heart in me, O my God; renew me with a steadfast spirit.** Psalm 51:12

Guard of the heart is the practice of releasing upsetting emotions into the present moment. This can be done by . . . turning your attention to some other occupation or giving the feelings to Christ. The guard of the heart requires the prompt letting go of personal likes or dislikes. When something arises independently of our plans, we spontaneously try to modify it. Our first reaction, however, should be openness to what is actually happening so that if our plans are upset, we are not upset.

The fruit of guard of the heart is the habitual willingness to change our plans at a moment's notice. It disposes us to accept painful situations as they arise. Then we can decide what to do with them— modifying, correcting or improving them. In a word, the ordinary events of life become our way to holiness.

Fr. Thomas Keating, O.C.S.O.
Open Mind, Open Heart

For Goodness Sake!

■ **God saw how good it was . . . God saw how good it was . . . God saw how good it was.** Genesis 1:10, 12, 18

Catholicism traditionally has been open to the goodness of the world and all of God's creation. A poem by Hilaire Belloc claims:

Wherever a Catholic sun doth shine,
There's plenty of laughter and good red wine.
At least, I've always found it so:
Benedicamus Domino!

The last line, Latin for "Let us bless the Lord!," expresses gratefulness for the good things of life and thankfulness to the author of creation. In its own way this poem repeats what the Bible says about the sixth day of creation of the world. God looked at everything he had made, and he found it very good. (Genesis 1:31)

At bottom the Catholic tradition is in touch with the goodness of the world and the joyfulness of life. It tells us to rejoice and be glad for all the great and small pleasures that come to us from God through creation. It has little in common with the Puritan belief that pleasure is sinful and that beauty is a temptation from the devil.

Fr. Richard Rohr, O.F.M. & Joseph Martos
Why Be Catholic?

Lord of life, grant me a renewed appreciation of the goodness of creation!

The Love Of Christ

■ **We can love God and never know a moment of untroubled prayer.** *Martin C. Helldorfer*

If God is for us, who can be against us? The God who did not spare his own Son but handed him over for us all, how will he not also give us everything else along with him? Who will bring a charge against God's chosen ones? It is God who acquits us. Who will condemn? It is Christ who died, rather, was raised, who also is at the right hand of God, who indeed intercedes for us. What will separate us from the love of Christ? Will languish, or distress, or persecution, or famine, or nakedness, or peril, or the sword?

As it is written: For your sake we are being slain all the day; we are looked upon as sheep to be slaughtered.

No, in all these things we conquer overwhelmingly through him who loves us. For I am convinced that neither death, nor life, nor angels nor principalities, nor present things, nor future things, nor powers, nor height, nor depth, nor any other creature will be able to separate us from the love of God in Christ Jesus our Lord.

Romans 8:31-39

Wisdom Of A Caterpillar

■ God wills to bring us to birth with a word spoken in truth so that we may be a kind of firstfruits of his creatures. James 1:18

A caterpillar becomes a butterfly by being a good, honest, healthy, reliable caterpillar; that is, by being fully and genuinely what it is now, not by trying to be what it is not. The better the caterpillar, the better the butterfly. The stronger the present, the brighter the future. The way for me to learn to fly one day is to walk firmly with my feet on the ground today. Nothing is achieved by dreaming and longing and craving and crying. Only by being fully what I am today can I get ready to be fully tomorrow what I can be tomorrow. My present stage fully lived is the best preparation for the next one. That is the wisdom of the caterpillar, and that is why it moves about contentedly. It trusts nature . . .

All growth takes place at its heavenly appointed time under the guidance of the stars on God's good earth. We have faith in the universe because we have faith in God who creates it, and we can trust its secret timings. Spring will come in our souls if only we have the patience to last out the winter under the cold snow. A good winter is the best preparation for a good spring.

Fr. Carlos G. Valles, S.J.
Courage to be Myself

God's Free Love

■ **Now my eyes have seen you.** Job 42:5

Job eventually finds solace in a new experience of God, an experience that was beyond his hopes: "Now my eyes have seen you."

The truth that he has grasped and that has lifted him to the level of contemplation is that justice alone does not have the final say about how we are to speak of God. Only when we have come to realize that God's love is freely bestowed do we enter fully and definitely into the presence of the God of faith. God's love, like all true love, operates in a world not of cause and effect but of freedom and gratuitousness . . . the Lord is not prisoner of the "give to me and I will give to you" mentality. Nothing, no human work, however valuable, merits grace, for if it did, grace would cease to be grace. That is the heart of the message of the Book of Job . . . human works as such do not justify, they do not save.

God is entirely independent of space and time. God acts only in accordance with the utterly free divine will; God does what God pleases to do.

Gustavo Gutierrez
On Job

O God, free me from my habit of thinking and acting as if I earn grace.

Loving As God Loves

■ **Scripture has it, "You shall love your neighbor as yourself." But if you show favoritism you commit sin.**
James 2:8-9

We are insignificant in comparison to the Infinite God. Yet God finds each one of us inherently and immeasurably lovable, good, acceptable and valuable.

Unlike the flawed love of our parents, children, spouses and friends, God's love for us is unconditional. God does not base divine-human relationships on how we look or what we do. We are all equally important in God's eyes. This was the paradox Jesus demonstrated when he emptied himself of divinity and came down to earth. He came to be my equal, your equal, the little child's equal, the prostitute's equal, the paraplegic's equal. We may have no use for such as those, but God does. Indeed, there is a sense in which God may be said to favor the poor and the outcast.

When we devalue others or ourselves we reject the wisdom of God who does not devalue anyone. The mandate for us as Christians is "to love one another as I have loved you."

Laurie Kozisek

Lord, help me realize that you love me and others infinitely.

Seek Spiritual Needs

■ **Ask, and it will be given to you; search, and you will find; knock, and the door will be opened to you.**

Matthew 7:7

I have a hunch that we will never walk away from our prayer disappointed if we yearn for spiritual gifts more than for temporal and material favors. When we ask for courage, trust, hope, forgiveness, acceptance, healing, we are asking for gifts whose seed has already been planted in the soil of our hearts. Asking Jesus for these gifts reminds us to connect with this gift that is already in our reach. It is a healthy way to pray. Seeking out our spiritual needs is an excellent way to grow up in our prayer life.

Can you plead with Jesus for the ability to forgive someone and not feel a tiny bit of love in your heart? Can you ask God to help you accept the death of a loved one without experiencing some kind of acceptance in the depths of your being? Can you ask the Spirit to raise up your own dead spirit and not feel a slow unfolding of wings in your heart?

Perhaps the real question we all need to ask is: "Do I truly want my prayers to be answered?"

Sr. Macrina Wiederkehr, O.S.B.

Holy Spirit, teach me to pray as I ought.

The Heart Of Healing

■ **Moved with pity, Jesus stretched out his hand, touched him and said, "I do will it. Be cured." The leprosy left him then and there.** Mark 1:41-42

In his encounter with Jesus, the leper in today's gospel experiences compassion beyond the ordinary. So moved is Jesus at the sight of this outcast that he instinctively reaches out to touch, to heal. There is neither revulsion nor fear of contagion. Rather, Jesus' response is a spontaneous outpouring of love, a wholehearted desire to restore diseased flesh and to end the stigma and alienation that accompany it.

Without deep emotional involvment in the plight of those who need our care, we are unlikely to be true healers. Superficial pity is not enough, and often professional skills fall short of bringing about the desired healing. Somehow, it is in the presence of a compassionate heart that we are most likely to find healing. It is in the presence of love and acceptance that the wounds of flesh and spirit are cleansed and bound up. When we try to offer comfort and healing without first feeling the pain of those who need our care, our words likely will be hollow and our gestures meaningless.

Elizabeth-Anne Vanek

Jesus, may I learn to feel the pain of others as deeply as you feel it.

A Tale Of Enemies

■ **I say to you: love your enemies and pray for those who persecute you . . .** Matthew 5:44

In Belfast, Ireland, a priest, minister and rabbi were engaged in heated theological discussion. Suddenly an angel appeared and said to them, "God sends you blessings. Make one wish for peace and your wish will be fulfilled by the Almighty."

The minister said, "Let every Catholic disappear from our lovely island. Then peace will reign supreme."

The priest said, "Let there not be a single Protestant left on our sacred Irish soil. That will bring peace to this island."

"And what about you, rabbi? Do you have a wish?" asked the angel.

"No," said the rabbi. "Just attend to the wishes of these two gentlemen and I shall be well pleased."

Fr. Anthony de Mello, S.J.
Taking Flight

Love Begins At Home

■ **Out of love, place yourselves at one another's service.** Galatians 5:13

Love begins at home. Nowadays we see with new clarity that the sorrows of the world have their origin in the family. We do not have time to look at each other, to exchange a greeting, to share a moment of joy. We take still less time to be what our children expect of us, what our spouse expects of us. And thus, each day we belong less and less to our own homes.

Where are our elderly people today? Usually in institutions. Where is the unborn child? Dead! Why? Because we do not want that child.

I see a great poverty in the fact that in Western countries a child may have to die because we fear to feed one more mouth, we fear to educate one more child. The fear of having to feed an elderly person in the family means that this person is sent away.

One day, however, we will have to meet the Lord of the universe. What will we say about that child, about that old father or mother? They too are children of God. What will our answer be?

Mother Teresa
Heart of Joy

O God, may I become more generous where we live and where we work.

Trust God, Not Feelings

■ **This will be the proof that we belong to the truth, and it will convince us in his presence, even if our own feelings condemn us, that God is greater than our feelings and knows all things.** 1 John 3:19-20

Simply because you feel good about your prayer doesn't mean it is pleasing to God. Simply because you think everything is wrong about your prayer doesn't mean you are failing to please him.

Most people expect too much of themselves. Everyone has difficulty with prayer. Even the saints at times found their efforts at prayer personally frustrating. Human beings are so easily discouraged. When you allow this to happen, you are being unkind to yourself and your prayer becomes less supportive than God intends it to be. He wants you to feel confident about him. His love is eternal and unfailing.

The Lord is kind and tender with you. Can you dare to be anything but kind with yourself as you travel your inner journey? Be at peace with yourself and live gladly because of the knowledge of his love. Good feelings are not always necessary in a love relationship. Love transcends feelings.

Fr. John Catoir
Enjoy the Lord

Lord, may I never forget your love for me.

Loving Others

■ **My command to you is: love your enemies, pray for your persecutors.** Matthew 5:44

We have learned that "love is an act of the will." But what about those feelings of attraction and sometimes revulsion toward those I am supposed to love? This is how I understand it: love is "the desire for the well-being of the beloved." To love, I need to do what is best for the one I claim to love.

We act out this definition with our children. We give them what is best for them, according to our capacities and resources. We do not always give them what they ask for nor, perhaps, at the time they ask for it.

My experience of a loving feeling is a natural way of being drawn to do what is best for others and sometimes I receive affection in return from those who love me. However I feel about it, I can still decide to do what is best, fair and respectful to those who love me as well as those who do not, just as Jesus commanded.

Eugene Skelton

Jesus, grant me the grace firmly and honestly to will what is best for everyone I know.

Peter's Weakness

■ **Simon, Simon! Remember that Satan has asked for you, to sift you all like wheat. But I have prayed for you that your faith may never fail. You in turn must strengthen your brothers.** Luke 22:31-32

Through Peter we realize that we have such a Master that even the most inadequate, the weakest, the most stupid, the one who has failed abysmally again and again can still be not only a disciple of the Lord, but can be united closely with the Lord in the apostolic ministry . . . The Risen Lord transformed this weak, defensive braggart from the Sea of Galilee into the compassionate father of the whole Church . . .

Peter is a source of hope for us precisely because of his weaknesses and his failures. Through these he can give us not only hope—the hope that we too can overcome by that same grace of the Risen Christ—but also joy in the realization that our weaknesses and failures can be instruments in God's hands to create in our hearts a deeper compassion.

Fr. M. Basil Pennington
Daily We Follow Him

Lord, through the inspiration of Simon Peter, may we never give up on your gracious mercy—even if we have, up to now, failed you.

Rich Man, Poor Man

■ **There once was a rich man . . . at his gate lay a beggar named Lazarus . . . the beggar died . . . the rich man likewise died.** Luke 16:19-22

Consider this Grimm folk tale, an interesting variation of the Lazarus story of Jesus:

Once a poor farmer died and went to heaven. When he reached the gates he was seated next to a man who was obviously rich. In a few moments St. Peter opened the gates and invited the rich man in. The farmer peeked in. A chorus of angels greeted the two with a rousing Bach chorale and shouting people filled the streets. Then St. Peter gave the rich man a welcoming speech.

When it was quiet, St. Peter opened the gates and welcomed the poor farmer. He was greeted warmly, but without the to-do afforded the rich man. The farmer was deeply hurt. He told St. Peter that all his life he had watched the rich get preferences on earth, but had thought all would be equal in heaven.

"All will be equal," St. Peter said. "You have to understand that today is a special occasion. We receive poor farmers up here every day, but we haven't had a rich man in more than eighty years."

William R. White
Stories for Telling

Evil And Good

■ **They sold Joseph to the Ishmaelites for twenty pieces of silver.** Genesis 37:28

I am sure you have heard the old saying that God writes straight with crooked lines . . . In the story of Joseph being sold as a slave by his brothers and in the New Testament parable of the vineyard owner sending his son to restore order, we see how God used the malice of some to bring supreme good to all.

We sometimes wonder where God's plan is to be found. We see natural disaster, riots and war. We experience sickness, suffering and frustration. At the moment, like Joseph, we cannot see why God tolerates all these evils, let alone how God will use them to accomplish some divine purpose. But we must never be fooled into suspecting that somehow God has lost control of human affairs or that evil has become so powerful that even God cannot draw good from it. Though it is true that God could prevent all evil, in divine wisdom God has chosen instead to write straight with crooked lines.

Fr. Charles E. Miller, C.M.
Opening the Treasures

O God, revive my faith and courage when I am tempted to see only evil in the world.

Self-Surrender

■ **Let tomorrow take care of itself.** Matthew 6:34.

It is a characteristically human trait to want to be in control —to be so efficient and organized that every possibility is planned for. Thinking ahead, budgeting our time and setting goals not only give us a sense of accomplishment, but also save us from tension headaches. It is only in times of disorientation when all our plans fall apart that we realize how powerless we really are. Then depression and frustration set in; then terror holds us in its grip.

Competency and planning are not in themselves obstacles to our inner growth, but they can make us forget who is God. We imagine that we can surrender selectively —that we can pick and choose areas of life which we control while inviting God into others. Surrender means accepting whatever comes our way in the trust that God will be with us, even in the most painful of circumstances. Surrender means taking one day at a time and accepting it as a gift to be reverenced.

Elizabeth-Anne Vanek

O God, help me to willingly accept this day all that comes—trusting that you will be with me.

The Fire Of Purgatory

■ The day will begin with fire, and the fire will test the quality of each man's work . . . and though he is saved himself, it will be as one who has gone through fire.

1 Corinthians 3:13,15

If I am to go neither to hell nor heaven, where shall I go? Purgatory, and it is most certainly this side of the eternal watershed . . . I think of the souls of the dead completing their period of expiation near where they lived, perhaps even in their own homes.

There is a fire, but not a material kind. To touch my soul another type of fire is necessary: charity. My soul will writhe, sizzle and smoke like green wood, but it will burn in the end. **Not a single fiber shall escape, all must be consumed by that divine love.**

How long will this take? Some people will need no more than a few days, others thousands of years . . .

All this will take place while a sort of film of our lives is screened before our eyes . . . No, there is no need for a coal fire: the fire of failed responsibility, of injustices, of thefts, of lies, of help denied to someone who needed me, of love not lived with those who were my brothers, is more than sufficient.

Carlo Carretto
Love is for Living

A Faithful Christian

■ **You must remain loyal to the Lord, your God, as you have been to this day.** Joshua 23:8

When God speaks to us and calls us, and we do the work of faith throughout our lives, and if we really love God and our neighbor through this faith—do not merely feel an emotion but love them in actual deeds of sacrifice—and if we are steadfast in hope because we know that we are pilgrims and that ultimate reality still lies ahead, if we practice this self-sacrificing love, active faith, and unshakable hope—then we are genuine Christians.

In the divine Spirit that is poured forth in our hearts, we shall then be able to endure joyfully the afflictions, the bitterness, the difficulties, the trials of our lives, of which Christians have not fewer but more than other people. For the Christian is a strange kind of person who simultaneously experiences tribulation and the joy of the Holy Spirit, which is deeper and more penetrating than any tribulation; joy that is strong and active and lasts.

Fr. Karl Rahner, S.J.
Words of Faith

Thank you, my God, for the precious gift of faith you have given to me.

Of Grubs & Dragonflies

■ **"Between you and us there is fixed a great abyss, so that those who might wish to cross from here to you cannot do so, nor can anyone cross from your side to us."** Luke 16:26

There were some grubs at the bottom of a pond discussing among themselves what it was like up there on top of the pond, where many of their brothers and sisters are called from time to time. The next one who is called agrees to come back and tell the others what it's like.

So this little grub finds himself drawn by nature up to the surface, and when he gets up on the surface of the pond, he marvels at how bright and warm it is. Then suddenly, he opens up and out, and becomes a beautiful dragonfly, which, of course, he was intended to be. He's flying back and forth across the pond and he can see them below. They can't see him and there is no way he can get back to them.

After a while he gives up trying and says, "Sure, even if they could see me they would never, ever recognize a beautiful creature like me as being one of them."

Fr. Jack McArdle
150 Stories

Lonely Road Of Pain

■ **Each heart knows its own bitterness.**

Proverbs 14:10

Simone Weil, that powerful philosopher of the human condition, remarked that the special burden of human affliction is that it cannot be shared with anyone else.

It is no one's fault that we are often alone in our illness. Others may truly love us and be worried about our sickness, but they are unable to cope with it. Some are better able to understand their own pain than the pain of those they love. Sometimes our loved ones are just unable to take up their cross of being with us as we bear our cross of illness. They are paralyzed by their own weakness and are unable to show us how much they care.

There is a great hurt from such apparent indifference, and it is a hurt that affects the one unable to help more than the one who needs help. Jesus recovered quickly from the pain of Peter's denial, but Peter wept copiously for the rest of his life, because he was unable to stand by a loved one.

Fr. Donald X. Burt
The Rush to Resurrection

Dear God, when I am called upon to bear the cross of pain, may I turn to you for help.

A Psalm For Lent

In your goodness, O God, have mercy on me; with gentleness wipe away my faults. Cleanse me of guilt; free me from my sins. My faults are always before me; my sins haunt my mind.

I have sinned against you and no other—knowing that my actions were wrong in your eyes. Your judgment I deserve; your sentence supremely fair. As you know I was born in guilt, from conception a sinner at heart. But you love true sincerity, so you teach me the depths of wisdom. Until I am clean, bathe me with hyssop; wash me until I am whiter than snow.

Infuse me with joy and gladness; let these bones you have crushed dance for joy. Please do not stare at my sins; blot out all my guilt. Create a pure heart in me, O my God; renew me with a steadfast spirit. Don't drive me away from your presence, or take your Holy Spirit from me. Once more be my savior; revive my joy. Strengthen and sharpen my still weak spirit. And I will teach transgressors your ways; then sinners will return to you, too. Release me from death, God my Savior, and I will announce your justice. Open my lips, and my tongue will proclaim your glory. Sacrifices give you no pleasure; if I offered a holocaust, you would refuse it.

My sacrifice is this broken spirit. You will not disdain a contrite and humbled heart.

Psalm 51:1-19

Learning From Suffering

■ **Whoever wishes to be my follower must deny his very self, take up his cross each day, and follow in my steps.** Luke 9:23

When I find something disturbing, that means that some attachment, illusion, or conditioning of mine has been hit; that is my chance to become aware of it, unmask it, and get rid of it. Thus suffering is the royal way to health . . .

All growth occurs through suffering, if only you know how to use suffering to end suffering. Don't distract yourself from the suffering, don't rationalize it, don't justify it, don't forget it, don't neglect it. The only way to deal with suffering is to face it, to observe it, to understand it. What illusion is behind this suffering? What attachment of mine has it inflicted itself upon? What conditioning has it violated? There is my golden chance to know myself, to check my weaknesses, to improve my life. Instead, we blame others for our sufferings, we complain against our rivals, society, the government, and even God; we escape into self-pity or bitterness or a nervous breakdown or try to drown our depression in hard work or cynical misery. If we learn how to profit through our sufferings, we will advance fast in our spiritual life.

Fr. Carlos Valles, S.J.
Mastering Sadhana

Fatherly Devotion

■ **While he was still a long way off, his father caught sight of him and was deeply moved.** Luke 15:20

How long had the father been waiting for his son to return? Did his eyes comb the horizon daily on the chance that the one who had left would return? What devotion kept him searching, hoping without the least sign that his child would come back? Simply as a story of the human heart, this parable is rich with suggestion and feeling.

If we understand the waiting father to be a representation of God, the story deepens. The Creator of the Universe keeping watch for one whose arrogance has led him away to squander his gifts and abuse his freedom. Even when the child is "a long way off," having as yet offered no words of repentance, God is "deeply moved."

I know I cannot understand such devotion, but I can try to believe and be glad such a God has breathed life into me, waited for me, and welcomed me back.

Mark Neilsen

O God, may I appreciate more deeply each day your loving-kindness for me.

Jesus Looks At You

■ **Jesus saw a tax collector named Levi sitting at his customs post . . .** Luke 5:27

Imagine you see Jesus standing before you. He is looking at you . . . Notice him looking at you. Notice that Jesus is looking at you lovingly and humbly. Take particular care to feel both attitudes in Christ as he looks at you: see him look at you with love; see him look at you with humility.

Both of these attitudes can cause difficulty. Many find it hard to imagine Jesus looking at them lovingly—their image of Jesus is the image of someone who is harsh and demanding, someone who, even if he loves them, loves them only if they are good. The second attitude they find even more difficult to accept—that Jesus should look at them humbly . . . Impossible! Once again, they have not understood the Jesus of the New Testament. They have never taken seriously the fact that Jesus has become their servant and slave, the one who washes their feet, who willingly died the death of a slave out of love for them.

Fr. Anthony de Mello, S.J.
Sadhana: A Way to God

Jesus, may I look at you lovinging and humbly, the way you look at me.

A Tale Of Brotherly Love

■ **I desire love, not sacrifice.** Hosea 6:6

There were two brothers who farmed together, according to a Jewish folktale. They shared equally in the work and the profits. Each had a granary. One was married with a large family, the other was single.

One day the single brother thought to himself, "It is not fair that we divide the grain evenly. My brother has many mouths to feed. I will take a sack of grain each evening and put it in my brother's granary." So each night when it was dark he did that.

Meanwhile, the married brother thought, "It is not fair that we share the profits. I have many children to care for me in my old age. I will take a sack of grain from my granary each evening and put it in my brother's." And so he did.

Each morning the two brothers were amazed to discover that their sacks of grain stayed the same. One night they met each other—and realized what was happening. They embraced.

Legend says God saw the two embracing and said, "I declare this to be a holy place, for I have witnessed extraordinary love here." It is also said that on that spot Solomon built the first temple.

William R. White
Stories for Telling

Self-Forgetfulness

■ **Then the just will ask him: "Lord, when did we see you hungry and feed you or see you thirsty and give you drink?"** Matthew 25:37

Those who are called the inheritors of the eternal kingdom are surprised by what the Son of Man says. They cannot even remember when they gave food to the hungry or clothes to the naked, or comforted those who were ill. When, they ask, did we do all this? The most characteristic thing about those blessed by the Father is that they cannot recall the very incidents which God seems to prize so much.

How can this be? The answer is simple, and easily understood by people who, without counting the cost, give themselves away in love for others. **The blessed cannot remember because in these crucial moments of their lives they forgot themselves**. That is why they cannot remember; they perceive human need and respond to others for their sake, ignoring their own needs, unworried about their own appearance, unconcerned about the impression they are making. The saved are those who pay the price of loving others without keeping an account of it.

Eugene Kennedy
The Choice to be Human

Just 'Saying Prayers'

■ **In your prayer do not rattle on like the pagans. They think they will win a hearing by the sheer multiplication of words.** Matthew 6:7

Anyone who thinks of prayer mainly or solely as an activity like thinking or speaking is woefully wrong. This is the case of those who dedicate themselves to "saying prayers" without regard for living lovingly in God's presence. For them, prayer becomes a human work, a product of our own which makes us feel satisfied and justified. May God forgive us and make us see our blindness.

But equally in error are those who, because they are so terribly busy, abandon prayer altogether or reduce it to something more or less sporadic, because they believe it's a matter of activities for which they don't have the time or energy. People like this will have to think about living in God's presence, feeling their being in God and for God. Prayer as an activity will then become easier for them, or at least more strengthening, even though they may not be able to devote as much time to it as others do.

Fr. John M. Lozano
Praying Even When the Door Seems Closed

Learning To Forgive

■ **My heavenly Father will treat you in exactly the same way unless each of you forgives his brother from his heart**. Matthew 18:35

It is not too difficult to mouth the words, "I forgive you." Our culture has taught us well when it comes to using the little niceties of social grace. But words do not necessarily say what the heart speaks from the deep. Words can cover and gloss over the real feelings I carry in my heart.

Angers and resentments from the past are like this. Because I walked away from the person and the situation unforgiving, the moment remains buried deeply, only to come out in another way at another time. On the surface it is forgotten, but until real forgiveness occurs, the resentments of the past continue to burden the heart.

Jesus reveals his mercy to me through his sacrifice on the cross. His way of mercy and forgiveness is mine to follow, if I will. If I choose instead to nurture my ego and pride, to sulk and feel sorry for myself, I am free to do so. But when I choose to act as Jesus showed us, forgiving from the heart, I become free. And by forgiving another as I have been forgiven, I learn a little more about the way of Jesus.

Lucia Godwin

The Will Of God

■ **I am not seeking my will but the will of the One who sent me.** John 5:30

There is nothing so small or so apparently indifferent which God does not ordain or permit, even to the fall of a leaf.

God is sufficiently wise and good and powerful and merciful to turn even the most apparently disastrous events to the advantage and profit of those who humbly adore and accept the divine will in all things.

I am aware that my direction is considered rather too simple, but what does that matter? This holy simplicity hated by the world is to me so delightful that I never dream of correcting it.

Let us be sure that God arranges all for the best. Our fears, our activities, our urgencies make us imagine inconveniences where in reality they do not exist. Our misfortunes and sufferings often result from the accomplishment of our own desires.

Let us leave all to God and then all will go well. Abandon to God everything in general—that is the best way, indeed, the only way of providing infallibly and surely for all our real interests.

Jean Pierre de Caussade
Daily Readings with Jean Pierre de Caussade

The 'Little Gospel'

■ **Yes, God so loved the world that he gave his only Son, that whoever believes in him may not die but may have eternal life.** John 3:16

This passage from John is sometimes called "the little gospel" because it epitomizes the good news in one declaration. And what a rich and fruitful sentence it is! Think about it. "God so *loved* the world." The good news is that the Father loves us. God wills to be gracious. Salvation is established and offered to us and to all for "God so loved *the world.*" The love of God is wide open, comes with no strings, is not hemmed in by political tests nor ethnic or racial quotas. It is not "a limited time offer," but remains eternally valid. God "gave his *only Son.*" God's self-gift, the Son's self-emptying is the proof of this love. Moreover, this "sending" means not simply the incarnation . . . but the whole paschal mystery. Finally, this passage includes both an invitation and a promise. The invitation is to faith in the Son, to "whoever *believes in him.*" The promise is rescue from death and the gift of eternal life, because "whoever believes in him *may not die but have eternal life.*"

In the face of so joyful and positive a message, who could fail to be moved?

Fr. Donald Hanson
From The Weaver's Loom

Sick And Tired

■ **Elijah said, "Yahweh, I've had enough. Take my life."** 1 Kings 19:4

Although Elijah was bold and courageous, there were times when he felt afraid, depressed and ready to give up. When his enemy, Queen Jezebel, threatened him with death, he moaned, "Yahweh, I've had enough. Take my life; I'm no better than my ancestors."

Surely it jars us when we read of a holy man like Elijah asking for death. But doesn't it also somehow console us? There are times in our lives when a series of low blows leave us sitting dejected and inclined to pray, **"Lord, I've had it—take me from this vale of tears!"**

Knowing that God's prophet all but succumbed to despair gives us some comfort when we have to face our own temptations to give up. We have saints and prophets we can identify with!

Virginia Ulrich

Lord, deliver me from the depths of despair when misfortune weighs me down.

Little Things Count

■ **Though I had toiled in vain, and for nothing, uselessly spent my strength, yet my reward is with the Lord, my recompense is with God.** Isaiah 49:4

How helpful it often can be to just step back and try to see things as God sees them!

We all have felt like failures at times. No matter how hard we tried or what we did, the effort fell apart or blew up in our face. That can be discouraging, especially when our jobs are involved or when we were trying so hard to serve or help others.

Yet, if we can somehow look at these failures through God's eyes, they don't seem so crushing. God looks not so much at the big ending as at the little steps along the way. Those little steps contain many successful moments. A hug, a kiss, a good work, a smile—given at the right moment. A prayer for God's assistance. A reaching out to another to help.

Rarely do we all fail at all these little things all the time. Most of the time most of us manage the little things well. And with God, the little things count.

Charlotte Rancilio

God, help me each day to see the good that you see in me.

Demanding Love

■ **I love God as much as I love the one I love least.** *Dorothy Day*

That we have passed from death to life we know because we love the brothers. The man who does not love is among the living dead. Anyone who hates his brother is a murderer, and you know that eternal life abides in no murderer's heart.

The way we came to understand love was that he laid down his life for us; we too must lay down our lives for our brothers.

I ask you, how can God's love survive in a man who has enough of this world's goods, yet closes his heart to his brother when he sees him in need?

Little children, let us love in deed and in truth and not merely talk about it. This is our way of knowing we are committed to the truth and are at peace before him no matter what our consciences may charge us with; for God is greater than our hearts and all is known to him.

1 John 3:14-20

Being Compassionate

■ **Be compassionate as your Father is compassionate.**
Luke 6:36

Compassion is derived from the Latin word PATI and CUM which together means "to suffer with." Compassion asks us to go where it hurts, enter into places of pain, share brokenness, confusion, anguish, mourn with those in misery, weep with those in tears. Compassion says, "You are not alone. I am with you."

Jesus is the embodiment of divine compassion in our world. He is Emmanuel: God-with-us. To read the gospels as fascinating accounts of sick and tormented people suddenly liberated from pain is to miss what lies deeper still, namely WHY Jesus performed miracles. In becoming enfleshed, Jesus experienced the vulnerability and weakness of our humanity, embraced it with the infinite tenderness of compassion and sealed his sincerity with the promise, "I am with you always until the end of time."

This is the challenge he offers us today: "Be as compassionate as your Father is compassionate."

Sr. Mary Charleen Hug, S.N.D.

Jesus, help me to be truly compassionate in all my dealings with others today.

The Brokenhearted

■ **The Lord is close to the brokenhearted; and those who are crushed in spirit he saves.** Psalm 34:19

Jesus knows how it feels to be brokenhearted and crushed in spirit. He wept over Jerusalem's rejection of him, he endured the agony of Gethsemane and he felt the absence of God even while he trusted that God would, in the long run, save him. By yielding to the will of the One who sent him, Jesus brought salvation to all of us.

As disciples of Jesus, we will not be spared broken hearts and crushed spirits. Sometimes we will find ourselves closer to God as a result of such trials. At other times, the trial itself may be that our hearts seem to have been broken for no purpose whatsoever. At those times, we have an opportunity for a trust in God that is supported by no evidence, no reason at all. Then God is very near to us, ready to save.

Mark Neilsen

Lord of all creation, help me to hope in your mercy and to believe in your presence when my heart is divided and my spirit crushed.

A Mixed Blessing

■ **You will know the truth, and the truth will set you free.** John 8:32

May God bless you with **discontent** at easy answers, half-truths, superficial relationships, so that you will live from deep within your heart.

May God bless you with **anger** at injustice, oppression, abuse and exploitation of people, so that you will work for justice, equality and peace.

May God bless you with **tears** to shed for those who suffer from pain, rejection, starvation and war, so that you will reach out your hand to comfort them and to change their pain to joy.

May God bless you with the **foolishness** to think you can make a difference in this world, so that you will do the things which others tell you cannot be done.

If you have the courage to accept these blessings, God will bless you with **happiness** because you will know that you have made life better for others; with **inner peace** because you will have worked to secure peace for others; with **laughter** because your heart will be light; with **faithful friends** because they will recognize your worth as a person.

Sr. Ruth Marlene Fox, O.S.B.

God's Glorious Gifts

■ **Praise God's name, and make known God's deeds to the nations! Sing to God; sing praise and tell of all God's wonderful works.** Psalm 105:1-2

The will of God is, in fact, our happiness. That's why God created us; to share divine life and love and happiness. It would be a serious misunderstanding if we were to associate the will of God only with suffering, loneliness and grief . . .

We are certainly doing God's will when we are enjoying, appreciating and being grateful for the many beautiful things God created—for good food, the moon and the stars, white sandy beaches, rippling streams and roaring oceans, the smiling faces of friends, the joy of a newborn baby, the encircling arms of love, the joys of success, the music and the poetry of the universe, rainbows and trees.

God has looked on all these things and pronounced them "very good." And it is God's will that we join in that divine pronouncement, that we use and enjoy the marvelous and delightful works of God's hand.

Fr. John Powell, S.J.
Through Seasons of the Heart

O God, I praise you for all your marvelous works of creation!

Good Can Come Of Evil

■ **They sold Joseph to the Ishmaelites for twenty pieces of silver.** Genesis 37:28

This seemingly tragic story of Joseph has one overriding motif which is stated at the end in Joseph's words to his brothers: **"Even though you meant harm to me, God meant it for good, to achieve his present end, the survival of many people."** (Genesis 50:19-20)

Mysteriously yet powerfully God brings our convoluted, mixed-up and even betrayed life to an overflow of goodness, even for our enemies and for those who cared little for us . . . A divine plan reaches into the depth of our existence. At times we may reach a clear but passing glimpse of it, other times we intuit it during long periods of prayer, yet always we are being directed and guided by it . . .

During Lent we should feel a renewal of peace and strength, a conviction that God's mysterious yet most real providence is taking even more effective control of our lives, so that we should acquire serenity even in the face of problems, disappointments and perhaps betrayal. "God meant it for good." These words must become our own.

Fr. Carroll Stuhlmueller, C.P.
Biblical Meditations for Lent

A Lesson From Nature

■ I solemnly assure you, unless the grain of wheat falls to the earth and dies, it remains just a grain of wheat. But if it dies, it produces much fruit.

John 12:24

Jesus reveals in these words much about the mystery of his passion and death, much about the ways of God that we find so different from our own ways. Do you think it strange, he asked in effect, that I must die in order to bring life? Don't you see the same paradox in nature, in your very planting and harvesting? Leave a grain of wheat to itself and it will never be anything more than that—a single grain of wheat, alive perhaps but terribly alone. But bury it in the earth, where to all appearances it is dead and gone, and that small, insignificant seed will amaze you with the fruit it produces. And so, he says, so it is with me, Son of God in flesh. "I, when I am lifted up from the earth, will draw all men and women to myself." (John 12:32) If I am crucified, if I die for love of you, then in God's mysterious providence you can flower to a fresh life; the whole world can come alive in a way reason could never imagine. If I die, you can live my life; the very life of God will pulse within you.

Fr. Walter J. Burghardt, S.J.
Lovely In Eyes Not His

Free Advice

■ **When Joseph awoke he did as the angel of the Lord directed him.** Matthew 1:24

A simple sentence captures the holiness of St. Joseph. So attuned to God's will was he that in the very depth of his confusion he knew a sign from God when he saw one. Should he wed Mary when she was pregnant with a child that was not his?

How many hours had he spent in prayer? How many days fasting? How many deeds done in the Lord's name? Yet he floundered still. He had no answer. He sought for it with everyone, everywhere. When he had exhausted all his best efforts, Joseph learned something we all must learn—grace is sheer gift, free as the breeze. It cannot be earned or bargained for. **Very often, only when the solution lies beyond our control do we free God to act.**

For St. Joseph, the answer came while he wasn't even conscious. In a dream God's angel told him to take Mary as his wife. Peace came to him at last.

Sr. Mary Charleen Hug, S.N.D.

Lord, help me to turn to you before my back is to the wall.

Living Simply

■ **My dwelling shall be with them; I will be their God, and they shall be my people.** Ezekiel 37:28

In the midst of a computerized, technological world that is becoming more and more complicated, many serious disciples of Jesus Christ are rediscovering the value of the virtue of simplicity. Striving to live counter-culturally, they are making valiant efforts to adapt a simple lifestyle with one view in mind: to follow Jesus Who is the Way, the Truth, and the Life. The closer a person is to God, the more simple that person becomes.

The saints are good examples of living simply. Blessed Elizabeth of the Trinity bequeathed her "secret of sanctity" to all who would accept it. Since the Trinity dwells within us, we have available the heaven of the soul while we wait for the Heaven of Glory. Loving attention, a simple gaze inward, a silent prayer keeps us centered on the one thing necessary in an otherwise hectic day. For all eternity we have been created to be a living praise to the glory of God. NOW is eternity in progress. We need only be attentive.

Sr. Mary Charleen Hug, S.N.D.

O God, how often I needlessly complicate my life! Help me to focus on my eternal destiny so that I may live more simply on this earth.

Leave No Loopholes

■ **The one who is not with me is against me. The one who does not gather with me scatters.** Luke 11:23

The attitude of mistrusting the incomplete choice and the halfhearted decision is just good common sense and sound psychology. To hold something back weakens the commitment and impairs determination. To leave a loophole, an escape, an alternative, undermines willpower and fosters retreat. I am not at my best when I know I have a second option, a possible retreat; I think that if the first course of action doesn't work, I can always fall back on the second, and that prevents me from going wholeheartedly for the first. The total commitment brings out the best in me; the cowardly compromise does no justice to myself . . .

Don't leave loopholes. If you leave them, you're sure to use them. **Ladders are to climb up, not to climb down . . .** to keep outlets for failures is not to have faith in myself, not to have faith in God. And to be weak in faith is to walk lame through life. Faith does not hesitate, and expresses its heavenly reassurance in its total irrevocable commitment. I believe—*but not quite*—means simply that I don't believe.

Fr. Carlos Valles, S.J.
The Art of Choosing

Prayer Works Wonders

■ **Be on guard and pray that you may not undergo the test. The spirit is willing but nature is weak.**

Matthew 26:41

We are very weak because we do not pray, we are deceived because we do not pray, we do wrong and foolish things because we do not pray. Our interior frustrations, too, and our faults, are in great part due to a lack of union with God. A soul who does not know how, does not want to pray, is as helpless as a fish out of water, as flaccid as a plant without sunlight. On the contrary, the person who is practiced in prayer and meditation can always find new hope and strength.

It is not virtue which creates prayer; it is prayer which creates virtue.

Learning to pray is learning to live. Prayer is discovering freedom, grasping the sunlight, tapping the reservoir of prudence, achieving constancy in good. Prayer is winning spiritual victories, conquering hatred, cancelling offenses. Prayer is harmonizing oneself with the peace, strength and joy of God.

Fr. Valentino del Mazza
The Patience of God

Lord, help me do three things more often and better—pray, pray and pray.

God And Creation

■ **You shall love the Lord your God with all your heart, with all your soul, with all your mind, and with all your strength.** Mark 12:30

God is not an object. God is not one thing among other things, and if you set God up in contrast to everything else you are going to have insuperable trouble. If I have to maintain the idea of God against the idea of everything else, I am going to have to fight everything in the universe because sooner or later some other idea is going to pop up. But the idea of God is not God, and God is not opposed to anything; God is not opposed to any creatures.

That is the real problem about some of the traditional books on spirituality where it is God versus creatures from beginning to end. If you get into that, there is no hope. You will never get out of it. You have to take God and creatures all together and see God in creation and creation in God and don't ever separate them. Then everything manifests God instead of hiding God or being in the way of God as an obstacle . . . here am I and here is God and here are all these things which all belong to God. God and I and they are all involved in one love and everything manifests divine goodness.

Thomas Merton
Thomas Merton in Alaska

The Death Of Jesus

■ **Jesus was lead away, and carrying the cross by himself, went up to what is called the Place of the Skull. There they crucified him . . .** John 19:16-18

Could not the divine imagination have discovered a different redemption, less difficult than death on Calvary? Couldn't God have simply forgiven us . . . If his Father wanted him to die—good God, couldn't he have died with dignity?

Frankly, I do not know the answer. I suspect no one knows save the God who invented the Passion. But one face rings loud and clear from Calvary: Where God's love is concerned, we mortals are terribly dense, dreadfully uncomprehending. We experience, day after day, what men and women will endure for love's bittersweet sake. We know that when the chips are down, if we love wildly enough, we will fling life itself to the winds for one we love. But we find it strange to think this way of God. Perhaps because the God of our education sits there like a Buddah, impassive, unmoving, hard as flint. Calvary cries more clearly than any theology textbook: We do not know our God. We cannot see that God was not content with some sort of legal redemption. He wanted to experience our earth-bound existence, to live our human condition.

Fr. Walter F. Burghardt, S.J.
Grace on Crutches

The Silent Minority

■ **Through baptism into his death we were buried with him . . .** Romans 6:4

During World War II, when American cities were blacked out at night, it was thought advisable to move some children of New York City to the relative safety of the Catskill Mountains. When they first arrived in the quiet stillness of the country, they were unable to sleep—**because it was too quiet.** So accustomed had they become to the noises of the city that the silence of the open country kept them awake. They could not relax with it. This might be read as a parable of today's society—it reflects clearly our uncomfortableness with silence. We cannot relax with it either.

Authentic silence is pregnant with words that will be born at the right time. Unless our words are born out of a reflective silence, they are apt to be curtains that cover reality rather than windows that reveal it. For silence can give us access to a dimension of reality that is too deep for words.

Fr. William H. Shannon
Seeking the Face of God

O Holy One who comes into our hearts and minds quietly and shyly, help me to appreciate anew the peace that silence brings.

Learning To Trust

■ **Jesus told him, "Return home. Your son will live." The man put his trust in the word Jesus spoke to him, and started for home.** John 4:50

With the simplicity that is absolute trust, the royal official placed his son's life in Jesus' hands. He simply asked and then went home. Imagine how much Jesus enjoyed this encounter of complete trust. For once someone let Jesus be God. No one gave him advice, no one questioned him, no one asked for an explanation.

"For once they let it all up to me," Jesus may have thought. He knew that at that very moment the color was returning to the sick boy's face.

Like the royal official, we can give God pleasure by letting God be God in deep trust. We simply ask and let go, knowing that God has everything under control. If we listen closely, we may hear God say, "I'm so grateful you put things in my hands once in a while."

When we think we have to help God by telling him how things should be done, we should remember the lesson of the apple: it's easy to count the seeds in an apple, but only God can count the apples in a seed.

Sr. M. Valerie Schneider, S.N.D.

It's easy to count the seeds in an apple,
but only God can count the apples in a seed.

Divine Love

■ You say you do not think you love God, and that is probably perfectly true. But what matters is that God loves you, isn't it? If we had to rely on our love where would we be?

Thomas Merton

Sing out, O heavens, and rejoice, O earth,
break forth into song, you mountains.
For the Lord comforts his people
and shows mercy to his afflicted.
But Zion said: "The Lord has forsaken me;
my Lord has forgotten me."
Can a mother forget her infant,
be without tenderness for the child
of her womb?
Even should she forget,
I will never forget you.

Isaiah 49:13-15

Knowing And Loving

■ **Jesus said to her, "Mary!"** John 20:16

When Jesus calls Mary by her name, he is doing much more than speaking the word by which everybody knows her, for her name signifies her whole being. Jesus knows Mary of Magdala. He knows her story—her sin, her virtue, her fears and her love, her anguish and her hope. He knows every part of her heart. Nothing in her is hidden from him. He even knows her deeper and more fully than she knows herself. So when he utters her name he brings about a profound event. **Mary suddenly feels that the one who truly knows her truly loves her.**

I am always wondering if people who know me, including my deepest, hidden thoughts and feeling, really do love me. Often I am tempted to think that I am loved only as I remain partially known. I fear that the love I receive is conditional. I say to myself, "If they would really know me, they would not love me." But when Jesus calls Mary by name, he speaks to her entire being. She realizes that the one who knows her most deeply did not flee from her, but is offering her unconditional love.

Fr. Henri J.M. Nouwen
The Road to Daybreak

Listen, O My Soul!

■ **Never before has anyone spoken like this one.**
John 7:46

Yes, Jesus, the Scribes and Pharisees heard you speak, but they did not really listen because their minds were closed and so they failed to recognize you as their Savior.

How I resemble them, Lord, as I fret and fuss, bent on telling you how to organize your world, my life and the lives of others. Or I am so busy listening to what is trivial or mere gossip, that I miss your voice pleading, **"Be still and know that I am God."**

Give me Lord, a listening heart, a heart tuned into you, so that I do not miss your divine voice coming to me daily through others, in my personal hopes and fears; achievements and failures; joys and sorrows.

Help me, Jesus, to achieve a silent, receptive attitude, for it is only then that I will hear your voice calling me by name, and having attained this close relationship, there will no longer be need for words, as a peaceful silence, pregnant with grace, will have come to birth.

Sr. Peter Dupreé

Be A Blessing To Others

■ **In your offspring, all families of the earth shall be blessed.** Acts 3:25

There is a story told about Bishop Walsh, the famous Maryknoll missionary. While walking in the countryside of China, he came up over the crest of a hill. There, straight ahead, lay the trail. Off to one side and out of the way he saw a village. He decided to detour through the village just so that the people of that place could receive the blessings of the presence of a baptized person.

Would that we took our baptism that seriously! Would that we had confidence that others could feel God's presence in us! How often do we think that the sacraments and gifts we have within us can benefit those with whom we come in contact each day? How often do we realize that, indeed, people can be blessed by us, that we can be channels of God's grace?

Eugene A. Skelton

O God, make me a channel of your grace.

Poverty East And West

■ **The Lord is close to the brokenhearted; and those who are crushed in spirit he saves.** Psalm 34:19

I find the poverty in the West much more difficult, much greater than the poverty I meet in India, in Ethiopia and the Middle East, which is a material poverty. For example, a few months ago before traveling in Europe and America, I picked up a woman from the streets of Calcutta, dying of hunger. I had only to give her a plate of rice and I satisfied her hunger. But the lonely and the unwanted and the homeless, the shut-ins who are spending their lives in such terrible loneliness, who are known by the number of their room and not by their name! **I think this is the greatest poverty that a human being can bear and accept and go through. . .**

The poor are hungry for God; they want to hear about Our Lord. They do not worry so much about material things; they want to hear that they have a Father in heaven who loves them.

Mother Teresa
Love: A Fruit Always in Season

BEFORE GOD WE ARE ALL POOR
—Mother Teresa

The Resurrection Of Jesus

At daybreak on the first day of the week they took the spices they had prepared and went to the tomb. They found the stone rolled away from the tomb; but when they entered, they did not find the body of the Lord Jesus. While they were puzzling over this, behold, two men in dazzling garments appeared to them. They were terrified and bowed their faces to the ground. They said to them, "Why do you seek the living one among the dead? He is not here, but he has been raised. Remember what he said to you while he was still in Galilee, that the Son of Man must be handed over to sinners and be crucified, and rise on the third day." And they remembered his words. Then they returned from the tomb and announced all these things to the eleven and to all the others. The women were Mary Magdalene, Joanna, and Mary the mother of James; the others who accompanied them also told this to the apostles, but their story seemed like nonsense and they did not believe them. But Peter got up and ran to the tomb, bent down, and saw the burial cloths alone; then he went home amazed at what at happened.

Luke 24:1-12

What Counts Is Love

■ **If I have all faith so as to move mountains, but do not have love, I am nothing.** 1 Corinthians 13:2

How idle seems our prattle about "believing" or "not believing" in God! Pure speculation, and more often than not, useless.

What counts is love, and so often we do not know how to love, or do not wish to.

I understand why St. Paul used such forceful language when he came to the heart of the matter, and explained . . . that all the glorious gifts of faith count for nothing without love.

So stop asking yourself whether you believe or do not believe in God. Ask yourselves whether you do or do not love. And if you love, forget the rest. Just love.

And love ever more and more, to the point of folly—the true folly that leads to blessedness: the folly of the cross, which is the conscious gift of self, and which possesses the most explosive force imaginable for human liberation.

Carlo Carretto
I Sought and I Found

Free To Be Saints

■ **If you hold to my teaching, you are really my disciples. Then you will know the truth, and the truth will set you free . . . if the son frees you, you will really be free.** John 8:31-32;36

The great tradition of Catholicism is ultimately a tradition of saintliness . . . Catholicism at its best wants people not just to admire saints but to be saints. It is a tradition that holds forth its saints as heroes and heroines because Catholicism is not something to know but a way to live. **It is a way to live fully and freely and lovingly, as the saints did . . .**

The reason to be Catholic, ultimately, is to be a saint. The saints who have gone before us point the way. They show that it can be done and how it can be done. Their lives are not meant to be slavishly copied, but they are given to us as inspirations for the future.They give us patterns according to which we can design our own lives on our way to becoming saints. Yet just as each of the saints was different from the others, so each of us can expect to be different from all the rest.

Fr. Richard Rohr & Joseph Martos
Why Be Catholic?

Jesus, often I am afraid of admitting that being a good Catholic means trying to become a saint. Take away my fears.

Messengers Of Truth

■ **The story seemed like nonsense and they refused to believe them.** Luke 24:11

We do not always accept news, even good news, from sources we consider inferior or inappropriate. And so it was with the Apostles. They didn't believe the women's account of the empty tomb. And yet, Truth was in the women's story.

The Spirit of Truth is not confined by our notions of propriety or seniority or rank or class or education. The Spirit of Truth is in the women's resurrection story, in the words of children, in the insights of other religions. The Spirit of Truth ranges more widely than we ever seem to expect. It is not our task to grasp truth in such a way as to try to control it. Rather, we should strive always to be open enough to recognize truth from whatever sources it comes.

Joan Weber Laflamme

Every truth without exception—and whoever may utter it—is from the Holy Spirit.

St. Thomas Aquinas

Trusting God

■ **My reward is with the Lord, my recompense is with my God.** Isaiah 49:4

God writes straight with crooked lines, the saying goes. At least, from the viewpoint of our limited human knowledge the lines sometimes appear crooked, often tortuous. But God, whose perspective is infinite and eternal, knows the divine plan exactly. When things seem dark, even hopeless, we need only to trust God completely.

Not even Jesus escaped that darkness. We sometimes imagine him as a superhuman person who walked through life with a prearranged agenda, as if life held no surprises for him. This is wrong. Betrayed and denied by two of his closest friends, he lived to see the apparent failure of his mission. Like the Suffering Servant, Jesus, at the end of his life, thought he had toiled in vain. But he was saved by his trust in God and abandonment to God's will. Faithful to his mission even to its ultimate logical outcome—death—he was raised and glorified by his Father.

Let us take heart from Jesus' experience. For us, as for him, God is our rock and our safe stronghold, and if we let go of our misgivings and trust completely, God will bring us salvation beyond our wildest dreams.

Nancy Benvenga

Faithful Suffering

■ **The Lord God is my help, therefore I am not disgraced; I have set my face like flint, knowing that I shall not be put to shame.** Isaiah 50:7

I feel very powerless in the face of all the world's problems. I want to do something. I have to do something. I have, at least, to speak out against the violence and malnutrition, the oppression and exploitation. Beyond this, I have to act in any way possible to alleviate the pain I see in the world. But there is an even harder task: to carry my own cross, the cross of my loneliness and isolation, the cross of the rejections I experience, the cross of my depression and inner anguish. As long as I agonize over the pain of others far away but cannot carry the pain that is uniquely mine, I may become an activist, even a defender of humanity, but not yet a follower of Jesus. **Somehow my bond with those who suffer oppression is made real through my willingness to suffer my loneliness.** But it is a burden I try to avoid, sometimes, by worrying about others.

Fr. Henri J. M. Nouwen
Walk with Jesus: Stations of the Cross

Second Chances

■ **We testify to this. So too does the Holy Spirit, whom God has given to those that obey Him.** Acts 5:32

When Peter affirmed his belief in Jesus before the Sanhedrin, did he think of that other time when he claimed he did not even know the man? Was he happy to have a second chance? What had changed Peter's inner self? Jesus was still the same. Rather, it was Peter's perception of Jesus that had changed. Before the crucifixion, Peter had expected a triumphant worldly victory, even though Jesus had repeatedly told his followers his kingdom was not of this world. It took Jesus' death and resurrection before Peter was able to comprehend what Jesus was preaching.

We are often like Peter. We believe in a God who will keep us healthy and solvent. When these expectations are not met, we blame or even deny God. But like Peter, we get second chances—and third and on into infinity. God is waiting for us.

Sometimes we may think our faith has been lost. Rather, it may have been changed. The change can be painful and full of storms, but it will develop into an adult faith, a faith that transcends a mundane vision and gives us a glimpse of infinity.

Joan Zrilich

Divine Visions

■ **Stephen . . . gazed into heaven and saw the glory of God, and Jesus standing at God's right hand.**

Acts 7:55

People who lived in Old Testament times or during the lifetime of Jesus seem to have had firsthand experience with the spirit world. Someone was always having a vision or being visited by an angel or hearing voices from heaven. But our lives seem supernaturally lackluster, and we feel—and sometimes say— that if these things were to happen to us, our spiritual life would be totally different, packed with more meaning. Witness how people flock to Medjugorje.

But could it be that all of us have had our visions or been visited by an angel or heard voices from heaven? To have looked into the eyes of a little child is to have seen God. To hear the voice of a loved one is to hear God speak. To know the compassion of a friend when in need is to have been visited by an angel. And heaven touches us in other ways: a rainbow after a sudden shower, a letter from someone dear to us, even the tail-wagging welcome of the family dog bounding to meet us when we return home after work. Ah! God and the spirit world are nearer than we know. Maybe we aren't looking in the right places.

Sr. Mary Terese Donze, A.S.C.

No Excuses

■ **If I do not perform my Father's works, put no faith in me.** John 10: 37

Are we willing to be judged by what we do rather than what we say we believe or what we intend to do? I find it hard not to excuse myself, saying "Well, I meant to . . ." Jesus, on the other hand, is quite ready to be judged by his actions and to make no excuses whatever. **Imagine being free enough to let our actions speak for themselves and not feel compelled to justify ourselves.** Jesus has that freedom because he knows he's doing God's will.

"If it were a crime to be a Christian," goes the old saying, "would there be enough evidence to convict you?" Because God is merciful, none of us has to be perfect to be loved. But the more we try to do God's will, the less we will need to make excuses and the more our behavior will show forth God's own life.

Mark Neilsen

Your Voice Guides Me

■ **My sheep hear my voice.** John 10:27

Your voice, Lord, guides me. Ever since I was a little child, I have heard you call me by name, beckoning me closer to you, inviting me to share in your work of transforming the world. I have heard and I have followed, Lord, listening to no other voice along the way, determined not to miss even the most subtle of whispers.

Your company has brought me joy, Lord. I have felt your presence at every step; I have trusted your shepherding. And yet you have not saved me from pain. Though I have followed faithfully, yet I have still stumbled and known distress. I have not escaped the thorns, brambles and cruel traps. You never promised me immunity from pain, Lord, but only the constancy of your love. Your hand holds mine securely. I know the tenderness of your embrace, and I believe a time will come for rejoicing.

Elizabeth-Anne Vanek

Borrowing

■ **Taking Jesus' body, Joseph of Arimathea wrapped it in fresh linen and laid it in his own new tomb which had been hewn from a formation of rock.**

Matthew 27:59-60

I had no grave of my own. My body was laid in somebody else's tomb. Was it fitting that I, Jesus, God's Son, be buried in a borrowed tomb? Yes.

I was always borrowing things. I borrowed a crib in Bethlehem to be born. I borrowed Peter's boat to preach from. I borrowed a donkey to ride on when I came into Jerusalem. I borrowed bread and wine to make my body move and my blood flow in history. I borrowed thorns, wood and nails to redeem the universe. Why should my burial be any different?

I will go on borrowing things until the end of time, until I have borrowed them all and made them holy.

I will also borrow you. You will be my tongue and my throat, parched. You will be my hands and my feet, nailed. You will be my head, thorned. You will be my side, lanced. You will be my body, stripped. You will be my corpse, buried. And when the borrowing is over, you will be my sisters and my brothers, risen and unspeakably happy.

James E. Adams

Believing In Jesus

■ **For they did not yet understand the scripture that he had to rise from the dead.** John 20:9

Mary, tell me what it means to believe in your Son.

Listen, I will tell you, and remember it well:

When you see a forest ravaged by storms, and earthquakes shaking the land, and fire burning down your home, say to yourself, I believe that the forest will come to life again, the land will be calm again, and I shall rebuild my home . . .

When sin has you in its grip and you feel utterly defeated, say to yourself, Christ is risen from the dead and I shall rise from my sin.

When old age or illness embitters you, say, Christ has risen from the dead and has made a new heaven and a new earth . . .

When charity seems to have vanished forever and you see people sunk in sin and treachery, say to yourself, they have sunk, yes, but they will return because no one can live away from God.

When all seems a defeat for God and you are sick of woes, say to yourself, Jesus died and rose again to save the world, and his salvation is already with us.

Carlo Carretto
Blessed Are You Who Believed

Blessings In Disguise

I have learned to be content with whatever I have. I know what it is to have little, and I know what it is to have plenty. Philippians 4:11-12

Blessings come in many guises
That God alone in love devises,
And sickness which we dread so much
Can bring a very healing touch,
For often on the wings of pain
The peace we sought before in vain
Will come to us with sweet surprise
For God is merciful and wise.
And through long hours of tribulation
God gives us time for meditation,
And no sickness can be counted loss
That teaches us to bear our cross.

Helen Steiner Rice
Daily Reflections

Merciful God, how often I tend to forget that daylight comes after the darkness of night! Help me remember that, and to keep in mind that you will always help me to turn my crosses into crowns.

A Docile Heart

■ **Blessed are those who trust in God. Revere God, you saints, for there is nothing lacking to those who fear God.** Psalm 34:9-10

Have we the faith, the stout heart, the humble mind, the docility to God's good pleasure to see in the most contrasting fortunes of our lives a chance to bring forth fruit for eternity, to prove our love for God, to be patient and courageous, unassuming and devoted? Or do we insist on having our way in what we offer to God? Are we prepared to find God only in the particular situation we have chosen? Before we know it, God has sent us a different situation; and we have not the magnanimity, the willing, loving, uninhibited prudence, to perceive God's call and our duty in the different situation, to accept it willingly, to get on with it, to be content with God's good pleasure for us. Anything that may happen to us can be accepted as a grace and a blessing. Of course this means having a heart that is well-disposed and humble, that listens and obeys. But why not ask God for that gift?

Fr. Karl Rahner, S.J.
Words of Faith

O God, grant me a humble, willing, listening and prayerful heart.

Encouraging Words

■ **He encouraged them all to remain firm in their commitment to the Lord.** Acts 11:23

These are strong words: **encouraged, firm, committed**. How often in our lives do we feel discouraged, weak and uncommitted? Is it possible in our time to be enthusiastic Christians or was that an attribute reserved for the early church? Certainly the world and our experiences are very different from those of the early Christians, but the Scripture is written for all times and all peoples. It applies as well to us in our day.

The key word is: **encourage.** We all fail and we all get down at times, but there is something that we can do for one another which we often find hard to do for ourselves. We can help to put courage into another person. It may mean listening when someone is down; giving advice; reaching out; or just a smile. But a spark, an energy leaps out, the courage that another lacks can be caught. From that will grow strength and commitment.

Sr. Ancilla Keinberger, O.P.

A Plea To Perfectionists

■ **Though my father and my mother forsake me, you will still accept me.** Psalm 27:10

If you tend to be a perfectionist, Jesus might very well be saying to you right now:

"Why are you worrying about your prayer? I am always here. I am unchanging in my love for you. Because of your repentance, your sins are no more; my forgiveness washes them away. Think no more about the past except to glorify my mercy. The future is in my control. Do not be fearful. You are not growing lax simply because you accept yourself as human. If you fail to achieve the level of perfection you have designed for yourself, be at peace. I have better plans for you, but I need you to be humble, pliant and dependent on my power. I will answer your prayer for personal sanctity in my own good time. Allow my design for you to be the measure of your progress. It is not my will that you become perfect according to your own plan. The Pharisees strived for perfection and look what happened to them. Many Pharisees called me an evildoer and had me put to death. It is my will that you please me by loving others well, by loving yourself well. In this, you will be loving me."

Fr. John Catoir
Enjoy the Lord

Darkness Defeated

■ **They killed him, finally, hanging him on a tree, only to have God raise him on the third day . . .**

Acts 10:39-40

You lived with reckless power, Lord. There was no timid tiptoeing about but bold actions done in full public view. You never stopped to think of consequences or allowed yourself to be intimidated by those conspiring against you; rather, you moved with the Spirit, proclaiming the word of life, liberating those who suffered from the grip of darkness. You were the hero, battling the monster of evil single-handedly; you were the champion of the poor, the one who spoke words of hope into aching hearts. But at the end, Lord, it seemed as though you lost. You hung on that cross like a convicted felon, bloodied and shamed . . .

Then, on the third day, you shattered Death and burst from the tomb; on the third day, you destroyed fear and despair. The intensity of your living not only led you to your death but also to new life. You have triumphed over all that shackles and binds, limits and constrains. Your Spirit is with us, now and always. You are Lord of the living and the dead.

Elizabeth-Anne Vanek

Living The Gospel

■ **Go into the whole world and proclaim the gospel to every creature.** Mark 16:15

In our own day one of our greatest needs is evangelization—within the Church!

Evangelization means, quite simply, living the gospel in such a way that others are attracted by it and invited into the Church. It is different from evangelizing, which means preaching the gospel and baptizing people into the Church . . .

What the world has always needed, and what the Church needs today, is not just the preaching of the gospel but the living of the gospel. The evangelization of the institutional Church, though, can never happen if it is left to the clergy, or even to a specially trained lay ministers. If evangelization means learning to live the gospel, we cannot pay others to do it for us. We have to do it ourselves. Otherwise we fail in our basic mission as followers of Christ, and the Church fails in its mission to live the gospel.

Living the gospel does not mean memorizing Bible passages or attending prayer meetings any more than it means memorizing the catechism and going to Mass. It doesn't mean having the answers and going to church but living the answers and being the Church.

Fr. Richard Rohr & Joseph Martos
Why Be Catholic?

April 18

Keeping Tabs

■ **I did not come to condemn the world but to save it.**
John 12:47

An old woman in the village was said to be receiving divine apparitions. The local priest demanded proof of their authenticity.

"When God next appears to you," he said, "ask for a list of my sins, which are known only to me and to God. If the list is right, that should be evidence enough."

The woman returned a month later and the priest asked if God had appeared to her again. She said yes. "Did you ask that question?"

"I did."

"What did God say?"

God said, "Tell your priest I have forgotten his sins."

Fr. Anthony de Mello, S.J.
Taking Flight

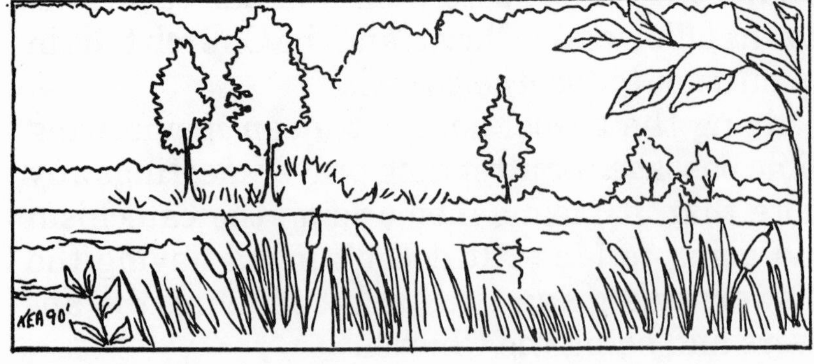

Christ's Victory

■ **We know that our old self was crucified with him, so that our sinful body might be done away with, that we might no longer be in slavery to sin.** Romans 6:6

There is no joy but in the victory of Christ over death in us: and all love that is valid has something of that victory. But the power of love cannot "win" in us if we insist on opposing it with something else to which we can cling, in which we trust because we ourselves can manipulate it. It all depends on who is in control—our own ego or Christ. We must learn to surrender our ego-mastery to his mastery.

And this implies a certain independence even of apparently holy systems and routines, official "answers" and infallible gimmicks of every kind. Easter celebrates the victory of love over everything. *Amor vincit omnia.* Belief opens the door to love. But to believe only in systems and statements and not in people is an evasion, a betrayal of love. When we really believe as Christians, we find ourselves trusting and accepting people as well as dogmas. Woe to us when we are merely orthodox, and reject human beings, flesh and blood, the aspirations, joys, needs of people.

Thomas Merton
The Road to Joy

Reborn Daily In Faith

■ **He took them to task for their disbelief and their stubbornness, because they had put no faith in those who had seen him after he had been raised.** Mark 16:14

The temptation to doubt puts our trust in God to the test. It can purify as gold is purified by fire. It can also cast a human being down into the bottom of a well. But there is still always light shining from above. The darkness is never total. It never invades the whole person totally. God is present even in that darkness.

Harrowed by the trial of doubt, all who want to live the gospel allow themselves to be reborn day after day by the confidence of God, and life finds meaning again.

The meaning of life cannot be drawn from the clouds or from opinions; it is nourished by a trusting. God sends this trust like a breath of the Spirit falling upon every human being.

One of the irreplaceable marks of the gospel is that God invites human beings to place their confidence in One who has come out of the grave and is alive. **Faith is not an opinion, it is an attitude:** the believer welcomes the Risen Lord and so becomes alive, not half dead.

Brother Roger of Taize & Mother Teresa of Calcutta
Meditations on the Way of the Cross

My Empty Tombs

■ **Why are you weeping? Who is it you are looking for?** John 20:15

What can I do with this story? Even as I pose the question, I know it's the wrong question. I have moved through these words and examined the message, but it is not enough for me to move through these words. **These words must move through me.** They must burn into my soul and awaken me. A new question forms in my heart and I hear myself asking, "What can this story do with me?"

It can transform me. From this Gospel, I learn the value of sacred sorrow. Only when I stand at the tomb of my heart weeping because of some great emptiness I've experienced will I be awake enough to hear my name when it is called. Only then will I understand resurrection.

This weeping-at-the-tomb story convinces me that the joy of Easter follows the holy sorrow of Good Friday. I must learn that I must attend to my sorrows. I must weep at the empty tombs of my life. In the midst of my weeping the beloved calls out my name and shows me what it is that I must stop clinging to if I am to truly experience resurrection. I must let go of all my false images of the One for whom I am seeking.

Sr. Macrina Wiederkehr, O.S.B.

Our Lady's 'Yes'

■ **"Let it be done to me as you say."** Luke 1:38

Our Lady said yes. She said yes for us all. It was as if the human race were a little dark house, without light or air, locked and latched. The wind of the Spirit had beaten on the door, rattled the windows, tapped on the dark glass with the tiny hands of flowers, flung golden seed against it, even, in a harsh storm, lashed it with the limbs of a great tree—the prophecy of the Cross—and yet the Spirit was outside. But one day a girl opened the door, and the little house was swept pure and sweet by the wind. Seas of light swept through it, and the light remained in it; and in that house a Child was born and the Child was God.

Our Lady said yes for the human race. Each one of us must echo that yes for our own lives.

We are all asked if we will surrender what we are, our humanity, our flesh and blood, to the Holy Spirit and allow Christ to fill the emptiness formed by the particular shape of our life.

The surrender that is asked of us includes complete and absolute trust; it must be like Our Lady's surrender, without condition.

Caryll Houselander
The Reed of God

Jesus, help me give an unqualified "yes" to the promptings of your Holy Spirit.

Skeptical Hearts

■ **Why do questions arise in your hearts?** Luke 24:38

Even when you, O Jesus, appeared to your disciples after the resurrection and showed your wounds, they were slow to believe. But you opened their minds, so the truth became clear to them. They were overcome with joy.

Jesus, at times all things seem to be clear to me. I know and I believe that you are the Savior, the Son of God, that you are present in all who believe in you. I am so convinced that for a moment I can truly say with all my heart, My God and My All. Thank you for those moments. But I ask you not to let my faith weaken in those times when you seem far away, in those moments when I forget you, or even try to put other things in the place where you should be. Let me always be certain that deep within me, you are present in the darkness, in the forgetting. I know you are.

Fr. Killian Speckner
The Prayers of Father Killian

No speck so tiny, no spark can be so dim,
The wise don't see God's splendor deep within.
Angelus Silesius

Bread Fellows

■ **I myself am the bread of life.** John 6:35

We are companions on a spiritual journey. The word ***companion*** has an inspiring origin—"cum panis," that is, "with bread." We are bread for one another, we nourish and sustain our fellow travelers.

To our intimates we offer the bread of friendship. For co-workers we break the bread of understanding. To the poor we distribute daily bread to sustain life. For the lonely and discouraged we slice the bread of compassion. Toward acquaintances we extend the bread of interest and loving concern.

Like Jesus, we are the bread of life, blessed, broken and shared. In the sharing is the gathering of fragments, those mosaic pieces that will one day form the pattern of all companions on the journey who form the one loaf, the one Body of Christ.

Sr. M. Valerie Schneider, S.N.D.

Identity Badges

■ **Look at my hands and my feet; it is really I.**
Luke 24:39

Jesus' wounds are the proof of his dying, the proof of his rising. As he stands before them, glorified yet bearing the marks of his agony, his friends can see and touch all that he has been through. No impostor, no ghost, would take on the burden of those wounds. No one other than the risen Jesus could bring such joy and peace, and yet be so scarred.

Wounds can be a source of identification. They are not to be forgotten, camouflaged or ignored, but worn proudly like badges or trophies of great price. They testify to who we are, reflecting all the physical suffering, the mental anguish, the emotional crises that have been uniquely ours. They proclaim that, like Jesus, we also have endured the time of great trial, that we have been washed in our own blood, as well as in the blood of the Lamb. They are our guarantee that a time will come when all wounds will be bound and when all weeping will be turned into laughter.

Elizabeth-Anne Vanek

Locked Doors

■ **Despite the locked doors, Jesus came and stood before them.** John 20:26

We are experts at locking doors. Our sense of self-preservation extends beyond locking car doors and house doors to locking the doors to our hearts. Just as effectively as we keep out thieves and vagabonds from our property, so we learn to keep out those who would extend friendship if we would only let them. Sometimes, we even succeed in locking out God.

We are so familiar with the invitation in the Bible to "knock and the door will be opened to you" (Mt. 7:7-8), that it seems strange to think of God knocking on our doors instead. In the Gospel today, Jesus, fresh from the tomb, doesn't bother to knock but breaks through the closed doors of the upper room and through the disciples' fears. In his presence, they find belief and direction, the courage to move back into the world. From this point on, life must be all open doors, and locks and bolts become relics of the past. How happy are we that God's love is stronger than all the complicated barricades we are so good at building.

Elizabeth-Anne Vanek

God, show me today the locked and bolted doors in my life.

No Greater Sweetness

■ **I myself am the bread of life. No one who comes to me shall ever be hungry.** John 6:35

Friend, you go through toil and labor, all for the love of what? Avarice—the love of money. That love always brings toil to its lover, but there is no toil in the love of God. Avarice will enjoin upon you the endurance of labors, dangers, wear and tear, and troubles aplenty. You will meet all those demands, but to what end? To gain what fills your purse, but to lose your peace of mind. Peace of mind! I dare say that you had more of it before you were rich than after you got wealthy. See what avarice has got for you: a houseful of goods, but much fear of theft; gain of money, but loss of sleep. All this avarice demanded, and you complied.

What of God's demands? Simply love me, God says. You may love money and go after it, yet may not find it. Whoever seeks me, I am there. You may love place and position, yet may never attain them. No one ever loved me and failed to attain me. To get by in the world you need to curry favor with powerful people through agents. No one need approach me through any go-between; love alone puts you in my presence. And there is no sweetness greater than that love.

St. Augustine
from *An Augustine Treasury*

Arms Control

■ As long as Moses held up the rod in his hands, Israel was winning; but whenever he rested his arms at his sides, the soldiers of Amalek were winning.

Exodus 17:11

Pray always and don't give up, we are told. That's a lot easier said than done, though.

Putting ourselves in Moses' shoes (arms, perhaps), we can almost feel the tiredness. How often we say, how often we hear, "I can't do this anymore! I'm too tired. It hurts too much." Ever feel your arms just falling? Ever have a feeling that a strength other than your own was holding them up?

If God expects us to pray always and not give up, God will make up for what we lack. Most often God sends support through other people. Still, when one is actually going through a sagging-arms period, the temptation will come to give up. We must then look beyond our own strength and trust God, who has promised to be faithful. We even have a familiar sign of that promise—the cross, when Jesus stretched out his arms in an ultimate prayer for us.

Sr. Ancilla Keinberger, O.P.

Perseverance doesn't come from our power, but it is within our power. St. Francis de Sales

Getting To Know God

■ **Know that Yahweh is God! Yahweh made us, and we belong to God.** Psalm 100:3

We tend to identify ourselves with the ordinary flow of our thoughts. But there is a deeper part of ourselves. Centering prayer opens our awareness to the spiritual level of our being. This level might be compared to a great river on which our memories, images, feelings, inner experiences and the awareness of outward things are resting . . . all are resting on the inner stream of consciousness, which is our participation in God's being . . .

Faith is opening and surrendering to God. **The spiritual journey does not require going anywhere because God is already with us and in us.** We must allow our ordinary thoughts to recede into the background and float along the river of consciousness without our noticing them, while we direct our attention toward the river on which they are floating. We are like someone sitting on the bank of a river and watching the boats go by. If we stay on the bank, with our attention on the river rather than on the boats, the capacity to disregard thoughts as they emerge, a deeper kind of attention will emerge.

Fr. Thomas Keating
Open Mind, Open Heart

Wisdom And Knowledge

■ **It's what you learn after you know it all that really counts.**

Our knowledge is imperfect and our prophesying is imperfect. When the perfect comes, the imperfect will pass away. When I was a child I used to talk like a child, think like a child, reason like a child. When I became mature, I put childish things aside.

Now we see indistinctly, as in a mirror; then we shall see face to face. My knowledge is imperfect now; then I shall know even as I am known.

1 Corinthians 13:9-12

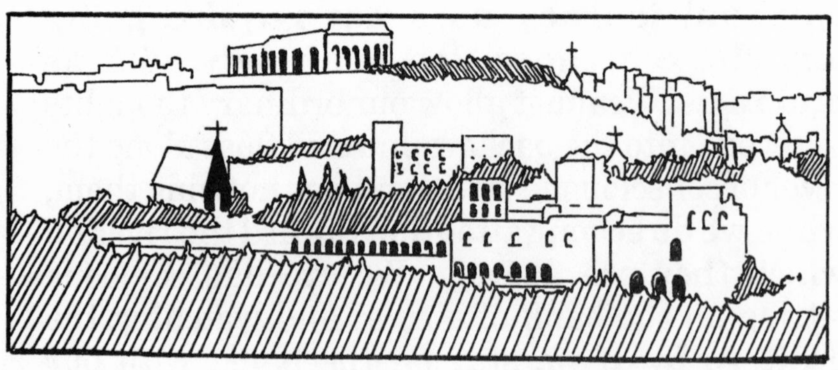

The Carpenter's Son

■ **Is he not the carpenter's son?** Matthew 13:55

Jesus Christ, Son of God and Son of Man, labored every day for many years at the workbench of Joseph of Nazareth, whom the Church venerates as a worker. Joseph had taught Jesus the work of his calling, set him to it, showed him how to overcome the difficulties arising from the resistance of the material, to draw works of human craftsmanship out from formless matter. **He, Joseph of Nazareth, linked the Son of God to human labor once and for all.**

Thanks to him, Christ belongs to the world of labor and he testifies to its lofty dignity in God's eyes . . .

May the serenity of the modest workshop of Nazareth ever reign in your workplaces, the serenity making human labor a factor for growth and giving it the dimension of a fruitful vocation . . . The Lord is always with you at your workbenches, to give all the regenerative power of his gospel, of his grace and of his love. Never ignore him! Never put him aside.

Pope John Paul II
Prayers and Devotions

Source Of Strength

■ **I am the vine, you are the branches.** John 15:5

In our garden was a grape vine, a sturdy vine which tangled so intricately up and over the trellis that it was difficult to distinguish one branch from another. I remember the heavy bunches of grapes, the sweet smell of decay as fruit fermented on the ground, the drone of drunken wasps, the endless jugs of grape juice on which we feasted all summer long . . .

When I read Jesus' description of himself as the true vine, I remember this grape vine of my childhood. I remember marvelling at how a single, gnarled trunk could support so much fruitfulness from June to October. I think, too, of my own "fruitfulness" and how dependent I am upon Jesus as the single source of all I do. I think of the countless others who also derive their gifts and their strength from Jesus and of the ways in which we are bound to each other.

Frustration and failure have taught me that on my own, I can do nothing. Yet, with Jesus, how much we can do! How fruitful we can become!

Elizabeth-Anne Vanek

Jesus, please show me today the ways I am failing to branch out because I fail to cling to you, the vine, the source of my strength.

Miracles

■ **Anyone who loves me will be true to my word.**
John 14:23

A man traversed land and sea to check for himself the extraordinary fame of the Master.

"What miracles has your Master worked?" he asked a disciple.

The disciple answered, "Well, there are miracles and miracles. In your land, it is regarded as a miracle if God does someone's will. In our land, it is regarded as a miracle if someone does the will of God."

□□□

To a distressed person who came to him for help, the Master said, "Do you really want a cure?"

"If I did not, would I bother to come to you?"

"Oh yes, many people do . . . they come not for a cure—that's painful. But they come for relief."

To his disciples, the Master said, "People who want a cure, provided they can have it without pain, are like those who favor progress, provided they can have it without change."

Fr. Anthony de Mello, S.J.
One Minute Wisdom

Longing For God's Love

■ **Live on in my love. You will live in my love if you keep my commandments.** John 15:10

Our honest opinion of ourselves is that we love God only in a half-hearted way—that, indeed, our love is often no more than resolution and intention to love him, far from that "with all your strength" that the Bible speaks of.

Yet, of one thing we can be certain. The person who has honestly resolved to seek the love of God may be said already to possess that love in his or her heart. For that resolution is a proof that the grace of God has descended into the depths of the person's heart to kindle there a longing for God's love.

What we must do is set no obstacle to the growth of this love within us, so that it may pervade our whole being more and more. We must ask God, the object of our love, to give us the sweetly compelling power of divine grace, to reach into the depths of our soul and set a spring of love there so that its waters may make fertile the dry and barren places of our lovelessness.

Fr. Karl Rahner, S.J.
Words of Faith

O God, I love you. Help me to love you more freely and more generously.

The Canticle Of Mary

And Mary said:

My soul proclaims the greatness of the Lord;
my spirit rejoices in God my savior.

For he has looked upon his handmaid's lowliness; behold, from now on will all ages call me blessed.

The Mighty One has done great things for me, and holy is his name.

For his mercy is from age to age to those who fear him.

He has shown might in his arm, dispersed the arrogant of mind and heart.

He has thrown down rulers from their thrones, but lifted up the lowly.

The hungry he has filled with good things; the rich he has sent away empty.

He has helped Israel, his servant, remembering his mercy, according to his promise to our fathers, to Abraham and to his descedants forever.

Luke 1:46-55

Sin And Sinner

■ **I call you friends.** John 15:15

How can prayer have any real meaning if people use it as a way to actualize a false self-image? Religion means doing the will of God, not one's own. Before getting down on yourself for not realizing some dream of perfection you have for yourself, see if the dream is from God. Don't waste nervous energy praying for something that God doesn't want. God never asked anyone to be great. He loves people, ordinary people, and that means people who bite their nails, people who exaggerate, people who are overweight, people who smoke too much, people who have erotic thoughts, even people who steal or murder.

God despises sin, but never the sinner. You must learn to see yourself as Jesus does, through the eyes of love. It is the work of the devil to fill you with the thought that you are worthless, rejected, despised. Don't believe it. Don't be anxious about your faults and failings or about God's love for you. It is infinite, personal and eternal . . . God loves you just as you are.

Fr. John Catoir
Enjoy the Lord

O Jesus, help me to realize that you are my friend and want only the best for me.

Recalling God's Promises

■ **I have told you all this to keep your faith from being shaken.** John 16:1

At night, it always seems worse. No matter what the fear or the anxiety, the long lonely night watch makes it harder. In the rational light of day, we can see some validity to all those truisms meant to banish anxiety. Most of the things we worry about never happen. Even if they do happen, we can cope. Look around and see how much you have to be grateful for.

But at night . . . All our fears come back full force. Stronger than ever come those tormenting "what ifs" and "maybes" of life, playing over and over like a broken record.

The only antidote that seems to quell these fears is recalling the many promises of love and care God has made to us. There are hundreds of such promises of love and hope in the Bible. Turn to them and you will be on your way to peaceful rest.

Joan Zrilich

Lord, when I am tempted to grovel in darkness and despair, help me remember your many encouraging promises from Scripture.

Awaiting Eternal Life

■ **Eternal life is this: to know you, the only true God, and him who you have sent, Jesus Christ.** John 17:3

O God, our hearts long for that eternal life which you promised us in Jesus, your son. You have given us the gift of life in this world. It is good and has brought us many other gifts. We have lived in joy in the goodness and beauty that you have shown us in your creation, in other people, in ourselves.

But the gift of this life, we know and believe, is only a shadow of the life you have promised us in eternity. We ask you that every day we long for it more. We ask that with every pain, disappointment, suffering, we will let go a little more of the life we see and touch and hold on to. We long for the day when we can put off this world, where we have learned to love, and come to you, where your love will be all in all for us.

Fr. Killian Speckner
The Prayers of Father Killian

God Is With Us Always

■ **Yet I can never be alone: the Father is with me.**
John 16:32

I can never be alone! That is the message Jesus gives to his disciples to help them gain peace and courage amid suffering. Jesus could face his horrible agony and death because he knew he was not alone.

As a disciple of Jesus, I can make this same claim. I may **feel** abandoned and wonder whether God cares—or even if God exists—when I learn of cancer, lose a job, bury a close friend or a spouse, get divorced or have all my life's work fail. Yet my mind knows that "the Father is with me." God's presence is the source of my courage.

If the Father's presence allowed Jesus to say, "I have overcome the world" just moments before his arrest in the Garden of Olives, then the Father's presence allows me to say, "I have overcome." Notice the present perfect tense—"have overcome." Even before disaster hits, I have already prevailed because "the Father is with me."

Sr. M. Valerie Schneider, S.N.D.

Eye-to-Eye

■ **If you really knew me, you would know my Father also.** John 14:7

An uneducated farmer who spent hours praying in the church of St. John Vianney once described his prayer this way: "I look at the good Lord and the good Lord looks at me." Could there be a more succinct definition of contemplation?

Contemplative prayer is a loving awareness of God's presence. We simply spend the time in a wordless communication with God . . .

Whenever I describe such prayer to young people, I have them engage in an exercise. I ask them to choose a partner and then simply to gaze into each other's eyes in silence. Inevitably, there is giggling and shyness. When I ask them how they felt, they say awkward, embarrassed and anxious.

The reason for their discomfort is the intimacy of this form of communication. The eyes are the windows of the soul, and to peer into someone's eyes is to see that person spiritually naked . . . In just such an intimate, silent communication, one's soul touches God deeply. We feel that frightening nakedness before God.

Fr. Stephen J. Rossetti
I Am Awake

The Power Of Evil

■ **For the prince of this world has been condemned.**
John 16:11

Disease, death, hatred and despair seem to gain the upper hand everywhere. Frightful evil exists. But will evil triumph? Jesus says no. He says that evil has been condemned to failure. Like a wounded beast, evil lashes out wildly and powerfully in its death throes. It is frightening to behold, yet it will not last.

What a difficult truth this is to live! **I don't believe it quite so much as I tell myself that I ought to believe it.** Yet if I act as if evil has been condemned and will be conquered, then every moment of my life will become an opportunity to hasten the victory. I could endure the dreadful headlines and my own petty faults with a sadness tempered by hope. I could view every birth, every kind act, every gesture of peace, every hand stretched out to those in need as a sign that the kingdom of God is emerging on earth.

I could even—Lord, could it be true?—be a source of hope and strength to others who grapple with the problem of the power of evil.

Nancy Summers

Lord, give me the grace to know evil when I encounter it—and to fight it boldly.

Life And Death

■ **Whoever would preserve life will lose it, but whoever loses life for my sake and the gospel's will preserve it.** Mark 8:35

We live well only when we are able to accept gracefully the fact of our own death and the pain of all the little deaths that are inevitable in the course of our lives. The uptight shall not inherit the earth; nor shall they inherit the Kingdom of Heaven. Though part of being uptight may be genetic, cultural or psychological, part of it is also religious. Wherever we may be on the "uptight" scale, faith moves us up the scale toward loose and confident and hopeful and graceful.

The old Catholic saying that we work like everything depends on us and act (and pray) like everything depends on God is true. **After we do the best we can, we simply have to relax and trust in God.** And if we approach the challenges of life hopefully and gracefully, then the part of responding to the challenge that depends on us can be done more smoothly, more effectively and with greater flair and elegance. We are all afraid of losing our lives, but if we can contain that fear we shall find our life more effective in this world and rejoice in life for eternity.

Fr. Andrew M. Greeley
When Life Hurts

With Jesus' Heart

■ **Whatever you ask in my name, I will do.** John 14:13

Could you order a meal in a restaurant for a casual acquaintance and have it be a perfect selection? Probably not. To choose just the right meal, you'd need to know a lot about a person—his or her level of hunger, specific mood and general preferences in food and drink. Imagine how intimately you would have to know someone to be able to perform this small service in their name.

To pray in the name of Jesus is not a matter of listing our own desires and then tacking on a magical "in the name of Jesus Christ, Amen" at the end. Rather, it is to pray as Jesus would if he were physically present in the same situation. Since the Resurrection, we are to be Jesus' "prayer proxies" here on earth, praying with his heart and mind and will. It would be too fearful a task if we did not have a God inclined toward us with compassion and understanding for every effort we make to pray in the name of Jesus.

Nancy Summers

Jesus, help me today to begin honestly and wholeheartedly praying in your name.

Brothers And Sisters

■ **This is my commandment: love one another as I have loved you.** John 15:12

A wise teacher sitting around the campfire late at night with several students asked, "How can we know when the night has ended and the day has begun?"

One eager young man said day would have arrived when one could determine which of two animals in the distance was a dog or a sheep. "A good answer," the teacher said, "but it is not the answer I would give."

A second student suggested the answer was when one could look at the leaves and determine if they were from an oak tree or a poplar tree. "A fine answer," the teacher said, "but not the one I seek."

After the students had discussed the matter for awhile and begged the teacher to answer, the teacher said: "When you look into the eyes of a human being and see a brother or sister you know that it is morning. If you cannot see a sister or brother you will know that it will always be night."

William R. White
Stories for the Journey

No Chance

■ **Then they drew lots between the two. The lot fell to Matthias who was added to the eleven apostles.**
Acts 1:26

I want to pass on to you as a simple but very, very important secret, a truth you arrive at after much journeying, after much thinking, a truth that makes everything clear to you in one or two words but is enough to solve huge problems which have bothered you all your life and around which you have vainly twisted and turned, wearing yourself out and complicating the simplest things *ad infinitum.*

This is the secret. **Chance does not exist.**

Chance is a word without meaning . . . a mere phantom, the erroneous solution to a problem, something accepted by the ignorant or the blind.

Chance does not exist. Unless by "chance" we mean what Anatole France says so well with this striking aphorism: "Chance is the pseudonym used when God chooses not to sign his name."

No, chance does not exist. The only thing that exists is God's will, a will that fills the entire universe, steers the stars, sets the seasons, calls all things by name, gives life and gives death . . . and wills the salvation of all.

Carlo Carretto
I Sought and I Found

Believe Your Own Eyes

■ **With a sigh that came straight from the heart he said, "Why does this generation demand a sign?"**

Mark 8:12

Jesus, I can almost hear your sigh. On some days I feel like the Pharisees asking for a sign. The earth is filled with the banners of your beauty, the glances of your grace, the fragrance of your faithfulness, yet I limp along in the heart of mystery never quite able to believe in your invisible visible presence.

With signs all around me I beg for a sign. My hands full of gifts . . . I beg for bread. My life full of promise . . . I beg for answers. My night full of stars . . . I beg for a vision.

The great St. Teresa of Avila tells us there are two kinds of visions: the kind you see with your eyes and the kind you see with your soul. The second kind, she says, is the greatest. Those of us who yearn for signs may be surprised at being encouraged to put more trust in our innermost soul than in our eyes. We would do well to ponder this deeply. **Make friends with your soul and you will not need so many signs.** Soul vision, when trusted and reflected upon, can bring about a deep transformation that endures even when the stars begin to dim.

Sr. Macrina Wiederkehr, O.S.B.

Out Of Control

■ **Accept whatever befalls you, in crushing misfortune be patient.** Sirach 2:4

One of the most difficult things to endure is being caught in a situation that is not within my control. A problem emerges and I become more anxious and stressful when I cannot forsee how the problem will be resolved. I do not want my life to be this way; I want to take action, make changes. Sometimes I want to go to sleep and not wake up until this—whatever it be—is over. I want to do just about anything but accept that these are the present circumstances of my life.

It is in this context that I must now follow Jesus. But it is hard. A dozen times a day I find myself saying "I don't want it to be this way," a kind of "negative mantra" that wells up in me without conscious thought on my part. And the truth is, as Jesus knows, that I really don't want things to be as they are. Only grace can help me accept such times in my life.

Joan Weber Laflamme

O Lord, help me see your will when I am in difficult circumstances, and help me accept what I neither want nor understand.

Dove Tales

■ **Noah waited still another seven days and then released the dove once more; and this time it did not come back.** Genesis 8:12

Children love to send balloons up into the sky, balloons with messages attached, which the eager senders hope will come back to them. Keepers at wildlife reserves band the legs of mallard ducks or wild geese to track their travels through hundreds of miles of chartless skies. And here is Noah, tired of rainy days, weary of watching, now sending out first a raven, then a dove to tell him whether his time of trial is over.

Three times a dove is sent forth. Twice it returns, once with an olive branch and then not at all. Noah knows he has found a place of peace.

If we have shut ourselves in, brooding over past problems, living in the darkness of remembered hurts or imagined fears, it may be time, indeed, to send forth a dove. Send forth a dove in the form of a smile to someone who has hurt or antagonized us. Send forth a dove in the form of a letter to a friend long neglected. Send forth a dove in the form of a visit to someone whose aquaintance needs strengthening.

It is springtime, the ideal time to send forth a dove.

Sr. Mary Catherine Vukmanic, O.S.U.

Sign Language

■ **I set my bow in the clouds to serve as a sign of the covenant between me and the earth.** Genesis 9:13

Rainbows are a sign of hope, especially in hospital rooms. When I visit patients, I see many rainbows on cards, balloons, mobiles and mugs. Other reminders of hope, of family and friends, are evident—family portraits, a favorite baseball cap, a signed poster picture of a football hero, or a crayon drawing from a loving grandchild. All these seem to give hope to the patient that life still goes on out there and that someone cares.

Sometimes a rosary on the bedside stand will be a sign of the relationship between the patient and Mary. At other times, a Bible or a favorite holy card will serve as a sign of God's love. Rosary, Bible, or holy card can remind the patient in a comforting, sustaining way that covenants are important, that relationships can be hope-filled.

What signs do I recall from the past that show God's never-failing love for me? What are God's signs of love for me right now? What signs do I use to remind me of my covenant with God? What would I take to remind me of God if I had to go to the hospital?

Sr. Marguerite Zralek, O.P.

Good Times And Bad

■ **Serve the Lord with gladness.** Psalm 100:2

Serve God joyfully! How easily that is accomplished when one is filled with Easter happiness! How quickly I respond when I am feeling good both mentally and physically! Gracious service flows naturally when everything is moving smoothly.

But service may also happen when I am not at my physical or mental best. My greatest work may even be done when my plans are thwarted, and the Holy Spirit leads me toward achieving something that I would rather not have done. God knows far better than I where my talents and gifts are needed most.

When I am challenged because I uphold some value, I serve God. When whatever good God has placed in me leads others to question themselves, then I can be accomplishing an important service without even knowing it. But no matter what circumstances arise in my life of service to the Lord, I have been chosen and must strive to serve God joyfully and unwaveringly.

Jean Royer

O Lord, give me strength in good times and in bad to serve you with a joyful heart and a quiet mind.

Disappointments

■ **When they heard about the raising of the dead, some sneered, while others said, "We must hear you on this topic some other time." At that point, Paul left them.** Acts 17:32-33

We all have disappointments like Paul's in our lives. We work hard, do our best and, somehow, the end result is far less than we expected. We lose our job to cutbacks or plant closings that are beyond our control. One of our children strays into an unhappy lifestyle. A spouse or parent must go into a nursing home. We are struck down by a serious illness or injury.

What can help us deal with these disappointments is the love that surrounds us from friends, family and sometimes even strangers. The source of that love is God. Through that love we are given strength, courage, hope. It tells us it is okay not to be perfect. And we do not have to be alone.

Disappointments are sometimes like a surprise package wrapped in brown paper: once we get through the hurt and pain of the wrapping, we will find a special happiness we never expected.

Charlotte Rancilio

Lord, may my faith in you help me see beyond the disappointments of my life.

A Message Of Love

■ **I entrusted to them the message you entrusted to me.** John 17:8

Sometimes, I take being a Christian for granted, Lord. I follow you out of habit and don't spend much time reflecting on the great privilege it is to share in your work. I get caught up in details and frustrations. I am bothered by my own imperfections and those of the church. I feel mute in the face of the world's suffering. I miss the point that I am not simply a laborer or a hired hand but a friend.

It is a matter of friendship, isn't it, Lord? One doesn't entrust what is precious to strangers or hired hands. Your message—the message you have entrusted to me—is a message of love. My task is to make that love known to all those whom I can reach, in whatever way possible. When I remember that I continue your work, then my hands are more deft, my feet move more swiftly and my heart is filled with willingness. Help me to keep your word and, in so doing, to give you glory.

Elizabeth-Anne Vanek

Surrender To The Spirit

■ **It is much better for you that I go. If I fail to go, the Paraclete will never come to you, whereas if I go, I will send him to you.** John 16:7

We have to surrender control of our lives and let the Spirit be given to us. We think that we might lose our individuality, yet surrendering to God actually increases our individuality. For once in our lives we are truly free to become ourselves rather than become what others want us to be. **The highest form of self-possession is the capacity to give ourselves away.** So by giving ourselves completely to God, we come to be possessed by God and we come to full possession of ourselves at the same time.

We experience the difference in our lives, and often others see it in us, too. We have something they desire, and yet we know that it is not ours to give. In fact, we do not have it; in a way, it has us. And it is something that they can receive only by giving themselves away, and allowing themselves to be possessed by the Holy Spirit.

Fr. Richard Rohr and Joseph Martos
The Great Themes of Scripture: New Testament

Come Holy Spirit, fill my heart with a generous and self-surrendering love.

A Consoling Presence

■ **"We were never even told there was such a thing as a Holy Spirit."** Acts 19:2

Suppose one day, just when you felt you had hit rock bottom and that life had little more to offer, someone introduced you to a man or woman who made all the difference in your world. He or she showed a deep interest in you and all your concerns and, without expecting you to compromise yourself in any way, promised to be always near when you felt the need for companionship or support or encouragement. You were delighted to find yourself so much at ease in his or her presence. For once you could really be yourself, could gain recognition for your good points, and could let your faults hang out without expecting a harsh judgment. How grateful you would be.

We do not have to suppose any of this. It is already a fact. The Holy Spirit is that warm and consoling presence, not only near us but dwellling within us, waiting to have us respond to the love and friendship being offered.

How heartening to pause and allow ourselves to be enfolded in that tender, protective embrace. Life may not be easier, but in the sweetness of that intimacy, we can go forward with courage.

Sr. Mary Terese Donze, A.S.C.

'Make Me A Saint'

■ **Be holy in all that you do, just as God who called you is holy.** 1 Peter 1:15

The church of God needs saints today. This imposes a great responsibility . . . to fight against our own ego and love of comfort that leads us to choose a comfortable and insignificant mediocrity . . .

The church wants renewal, but that does not mean changing a habit and a few prayers. Renewal is faithfulness to a spirit . . . which seeks holiness by means of a poor and humble life, the exercise of sincere and patient charity, spontaneous sacrifice and generosity of heart.

We should always ask Jesus, "Make me a saint according to your own heart, meek and humble" . . . Never stoop lower than the ideal. Let nothing satisfy you but God.

Let us thank God for showering love on us, in so many ways and in so many places. Let us in return, as an act of gratitude and adoration, determine to be holy because God is holy.

Mother Teresa
Jesus, The Word To Be Spoken

Jesus, help me overcome my fear of praying, 'Make me a saint.'

The Goal Of Meditation

I will meditate on your precepts and consider your ways. Psalm 119:15

We must be ready to cooperate not only with graces that console, but with graces that humiliate us. Not only with lights that exalt us, but with lights that blast our self-complacency. Much of our coldness and dryness in prayer may well be a kind of unconscious defense against grace. Without realizing it, we allow ourselves to de-sensitize our soul so that we cannot perceive graces which we intuitively foresee may prove to be painful.

Meditation is, we must remember, always to be associated in practice with abandonment to the will and action of God. It goes hand in hand with self-renunciation and with obedience to the Holy Spirit. Meditation that does not seek to bring us fully into conformity with God's will must naturally remain sterile and abstract. But any sincere interior prayer that really seeks this one, all important end—our conformity to God's will in our regard—cannot fail to be rewarded by grace. It will prove, without question, to be one of the most sanctifying forces in our lives.

Thomas Merton
Spiritual Direction and Meditation

A Bosom Friend

■ **No one can develop freely in this world and find a full life without feeling understood by at least one person.** *Paul Tournier*

A kind mouth multiplies friends,
and gracious lips prompt friendly greetings.
Let your acquaintances be many,
but one in a thousand your confidant.
When you gain a friend, first test that one,
and be not too ready to trust.
For one sort of friend is a friend when it is easy,
but not a friend when you are in distress.
Another is a friend who becomes an enemy,
and tells of the quarrel to your shame.
Another is a friend, a boon companion,
who will not be with you when sorrow comes . . .
A faithful friend is a sturdy shelter;
those who find one find a treasure.
A faithful friend is beyond price.
A faithful friend is a life-saving remedy.

Sirach 6:5-10,14-16

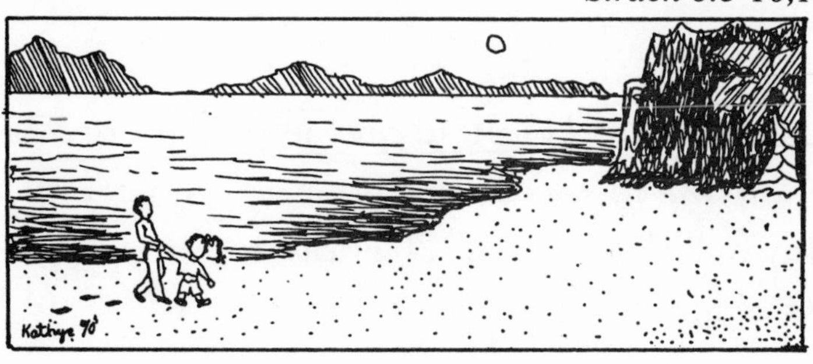

Joy—Now And Later

■ **You will weep and mourn while the world rejoices; you will grieve for a time, but your grief will be turned into joy . . . a joy no one can take from you.**

John 16:20, 22

Joy is not simply a matter of temperament. In the service of God and others, it is always hard to be joyful—all the more reason why we should try to acquire it and make it grow in our hearts.

Joy is prayer; joy is strength; joy is love; joy is a net of love by which we catch others. God loves a cheerful giver. **She gives most who gives with joy.** If in your work you have difficulties and you accept them with joy, with a big smile—in this, like in any other thing—people will see your good works and glorify the Father. The best way to show your gratitude is to accept everything with joy. A joyful heart is the normal result of a heart burning with love.

Mother Teresa
Total Surrender

Jesus, when I want to give in to discouragement help me to remember your solemn promise that joy will be mine if I endure the ups and downs of life.

Hopes And Fears

■ **Stay awake, for you know neither the day nor the hour.** Matthew 25:13

There was a very rich man once who knew a priest who was supposed to have a hot-line to God. So he approached the priest discreetly and said. "Father, if you find out something for me, I will contribute to the completion of the renovation of your church." Now holy as he was, he was practical and the idea of getting the debt cleared was very tempting. So he went along with the rich man, who asked, "Can you find out for me whether or not I'll be going to heaven when I die?"

Some days later, when the two met, the man asked, "Have you any news for me?" The priest answered, "Yes, but I have good news and bad news. Which do you want first?" He asked to hear the good news first.

The priest announced: "The good news is that, yes, indeed, you are going to heaven when you die." "Yipee! That's great . . . but what's the bad news?" The priest said, "The bad news is you're going tonight."

Fr. Jack McArdle
150 Stories

Jesus, I am like most people who want to go to heaven but don't want to die. I pray for the courage to live or to die well.

Dropping Illusions

■ "Go and sell what you have and give to the poor; you will then have a treasure in heaven. After that come and follow me." At these words the man's face fell. He went away sad, for he had many possessions.

Mark 10:21-22

I have been taught to believe that I cannot be happy without money. That is an illusion. Drop the illusion and you'll feel happy without money, as many people indeed are . . . Drop the illusions . . . the illusion that you need this person, this thing, this result, this event, this circumstance, this reaction, this security, this certainty in order to be happy. These are only illusions created in the mind by indoctrination and habit.

Drop . . . the well-meant brainwashing to which we have been submitted from childhood for our own good, and which has instead caused our ruin. Drop the illusions. **Nothing is necessary.** Once you break free from the internal compulsion that had made you believe those things were necessary, you will be surprised to find how easily you can live without them.

Fr. Carlos G. Valles, S.J.
Mastering Sadhana

The Laws Of Giving

■ **Complete possession is proved only by giving. All you are unable to give possesses you.**

Andre'Gide

Appear not before the Lord empty-handed, for all that you offer is in fulfillment of the precepts.

The just man's offering enriches the altar and rises as a sweet odor before the Most High. The just man's sacrifice is most pleasing, nor will it ever be forgotten.

In generous spirit pay homage to the Lord, be not sparing in freewill gifts. With each contribution show a cheerful countenance, and pay your tithes in a spirit of joy.

Give to the Most High as he has given to you, generously, according to your means. For the Lord is one who always repays, and he will give back to you sevenfold.

Sirach 35:4-10

Bonds Of Faith

■ **Mary remained with Elizabeth about three months and then returned home.** Luke 1:56

How deeply moving is this story of Mary and Elizabeth sharing their awesome news together! God offers Mary an intimate friend with whom she can share what seems incommunicable. Elizabeth, like Mary, has experienced divine intervention and has been called to a response of faith. She can be with Mary in a way no one else possibly could. Amid an unbelieving, doubting, pragmatic and cynical world, two women meet each other and affirm in each other the promise given to them. For three months Mary and Elizabeth are linked and encourage each other to truly accept the motherhood given to them. Neither had to wait in isolation. **They could wait together and so deepen in each other their faith in God.**

This surely is the rationale for Christian friendship and community. How can I ever let God's grace fully work in my life unless I live with people who can affirm it, deepen it and strengthen it? We cannot live this new life of faith alone. God does not want to isolate us when grace comes. Instead, God wants us to be linked.

Fr. Henri J. M. Nouwen
The Road to Daybreak

Called To Holiness

■ **God has saved us and has called us to a holy life, not because of any merit of ours but according to his own design—the grace held out to us in Christ Jesus before the world began.** 2 Timothy 1:9

We should have respect for cultural diversity. We should love those of different ethnic backgrounds and we should serve those in need, without discrimination. We should see ourselves as members of the universal Church and the world community. We must understand the implications of justice and mercy. We should foster a social consciousness which will help us to meet the needs of our neighbors, and to discern and seek to remove the sources of injustice in society.

No human anxiety or sorrow should leave the disciples of Jesus Christ indifferent.

But the world needs more than just social reformers. It needs saints. Holiness is not the privilege of a few; it is a gift offered to all. The call to holiness is addressed to all Catholics, to all Christians. To doubt this is to misjudge Christ's intentions.

Pope John Paul II
Homily, New Orleans, 9/12/'87

Jesus, I believe I am called to holiness. Help me to overcome the doubts I may have.

Love Of God And Money

■ **You shall love the Lord your God with all your heart, with all your soul, with all your mind, and with all your strength.** Mark 12:30

It is impossible to continue in contact with the realm of the spirit unless we give of our material substance for religious purposes. It is nonsense to say that we want the realm of the spirit and its power, that we are giving our lives utterly to God for this purpose, and then spend most of our financial resources on ourselves and our own desires and interests. It is worse than nonsense; it is hypocrisy, and God does not have much truck with hypocrites.

The spiritual realm closes and remains closed, except for occasional flashes of lightning, to those who do not give. Money is simply our congealed lives, what the world pays us for what it thinks we are worth. Unless we give of it for outer religious purposes—to institutions which, however inadequately they are performing, are dedicated to the realm of the spirit—religious encounter goes dead within us.

Morton Kelsey
Encounter with God

O God, forgive me when I say I love you but refuse to be generous with my money.

No Room For Selfishness

■ **There will be terrible times in the last days. Men will be lovers of self and of money, proud, arrogant, abusive . . . lovers of pleasure rather than of God.**

2 Timothy 3:1-2,4

To understand ourselves as members of a community, as individuals linked together to make up the People of God, as persons with responsibility for others is a great insight—an insight that is necessary for fulfilling our mission properly . . .

In the Church there are many different gifts. There is room for many different cultures and ways of doing things. But there is no room in the Church for selfishness. There is no room in the world for selfishness. It destroys the meaning of life; it destroys the meaning of love; it reduces people to a subhuman level . . .

There is a special and pitiable form of poverty—the poverty of selfishness, the poverty of those who have and will not share, of those who could be rich by giving but choose to be poor by keeping everything they have.

Pope John Paul II
Homily, New Orleans, 9/12/'87

When people are wrapped up in themselves, they make pretty small packages. John Ruskin

Prayer Of Petition

■ **When he heard about Jesus, he sent some Jewish elders to him, asking him to come and save the life of his servant.** Luke 7:3

Many of our prayers are prayers of petition, and people seem to think that petition is the lowest level of prayer; then comes gratitude, then praise.

But in fact it is gratitude and praise that are expressions of a lower relationship. **On our level of half-belief it is easier to sing hymns of praise or to thank God than to trust God enough to ask something with faith.** Even people who believe half-heartedly can turn to thank God when something nice comes their way; and there are moments of elation when everyone can sing to God.

But it is much more difficult to have such undivided faith as to ask with one's whole heart and whole mind with complete confidence. No one should look askance at petition, because the ability to say prayers of petition is a test of the reality of our faith.

Metropolitan Anthony
Living Prayer

O God, may I always have the faith and confidence I need to ask you for what I need.

Shedding Light

■ **You are the light of the world.** Matthew 5:14

There is a lovely church in a valley in Switzerland that has no electricity. At the end of each pew, next to the pulpit and lectern, and around the altar are candlesticks, with no candles. Whenever an evening service is held, every worshipper and each of the clergy bring lighted candles. As each enters the church the glow becomes brighter and brighter, until the nave is bathed in a gentle light. If even one family is absent, its pew goes unlighted, and the total effect is diminished. Each family knows its light is necessary to illuminate the church; everyone is needed.

We know that one of our greatest human needs is to be needed! Somehow we must believe that someone counts on us, that we are necessary somewhere! In this modern world of mass everything, we find it hard to believe in our own individual importance. But we must or we shrivel up and die. Our light goes out.

A. Philip Parham
Letting God

Heart-to-Heart

■ **The love of God has been poured out in our hearts through the Holy Spirit who has been given to us.**

Romans 5:5

Jesus, we believe that the Father loves us because we have welcomed you into our hearts as a Lord and Master. You tell us to ask God for everything in your name. We ask the Merciful One to keep us from sin, to change our hearts so that we want what God wants in everything in our lives.

We ask to see before us always God's love, flowing like a river, so that our love for others, our love for all creatures, will be renewed and refreshed.

We ask that divine love flow from our hearts into the hearts of all around us, especially those we live with and are close to. We ask that our thoughts, words and actions be infused with divine love, so that all the world will be drawn to praise, serve and love God.

Fr. Killian Speckner
The Prayers of Father Killian

Prayer When Disturbed

■ **Your law, Yahweh, is perfect, it refreshes the soul. Your rule is to be trusted, it gives wisdom to the simple. Your precepts, Yahweh, are right, they gladden the heart. Your command is clear, it gives light to the eyes.** Psalm 19:8-9

Each time I meet misunderstanding or criticism or even rejection, I am forced to ask myself why I am really working. Is it for me or for the Lord? If it is for the Lord, why am I so disturbed that my own feelings are hurt?

I have discovered that the prayer I most often find myself saying goes like this: **"Lord, let me be just as disturbed about this situation (or this person's behavior) as you are, no more and no less. If you are angry, let me be angry too. But if you are not disturbed, let me share your peace."** It is amazing, and quite humbling, how often my disturbance simply dissolves once I say that prayer and really mean it. Humbling because it makes very clear how much of my distress comes from myself, from my own wounded self-love and my own self-righteousness.

Fr. Thomas H. Green, S.J.
Darkness in the Marketplace

Searching For Jesus

■ **As they were returning at the end of the feast, the child Jesus remained behind unknown to his parents.**
Luke 2:43

The incident recorded by Luke in his Gospel is often referred to as "the child Jesus lost in the Temple." Actually, Jesus was not lost! He knew very well where he was—right where he wanted to be. His parents had gone on their way without making sure that Jesus was with them.

I have often done the very same thing. I make my wonderful plans, proceed self-assuredly with a project and then suddenly become aware that I feel quite alone. Only then do I remember to ask, "Where is Jesus? Why do I feel abandoned by God? Where are You?" And then I have to retrace my steps to the place where I sauntered off in my own direction. I will find Jesus waiting for me in the Temple—where I left him behind. Jesus will always come along with me if I remember to give the invitation.

Sr. Ruth Marlene Fox, O.S.B.

Mother of God, may your example lead me to drop everything and search for Jesus the moment I find him missing in my life.

Facing The Truth

■ **Where are your charitable deeds now? Where are your virtuous acts? See! Your true character is finally showing itself!** Tobit 2:14

God knows who I am. I do not need to pretend with God or cover up with flowery words in prayer. Through and through, God already knows me, sees in me what I do not want to see, and loves me in spite of the darkness and weakness of my being.

A film called *The Picture of Dorian Gray*, popular some years ago, told the story of a handsome but selfish man who had a portrait of himself hanging in his lavish mansion. Over the years, the picture began to change and reflect what was actually occuring in Dorian Gray's soul. The ugliness of sin and evil gradually replaced the face of the handsome, young man.

This film continues to remind me that while I may pretend with others or even with myself, my true portrait hangs before God who knows me just as I am. Still, it is difficult to face myself honestly, to look at the good and ugly in me and accept and love myself as I am. But if I am good enough for God, that's good enough for me.

Lucia Godwin

Disarming Distractions

■ **Better a handful of quietness than two hands full of toil and a striving after wind.** Ecclesiastes 4:6

What about distractions in meditation . . .?

A little story might be helpful. Imagine yourself sitting in a room with two doors; this room is your mind. You begin to meditate and immediately there is a loud banging on the doors. Sure, it is a flood of distractions trying to get in.

If you do everything you can to keep the door shut, naturally the distractions will only pound on the door all the louder. What ensues is a terrible racket and a great strain on the nerves. You become mentally tired trying to hold the door closed and keeping the distractions out. The result? You become tired, frustrated and frazzled. And the thoughts that were trying to get in have really become distractions because you spent your entire time with them instead of with the Lord.

What to do? Open the door. Yes, just let them in . . . But do not stop there. Once inside the room, do not latch onto them . . . *Let them come in one door and go directly out the other.* There will be a train of thoughts flowing from one door to the other, but it will be a smooth flow which does not distract nor cause tension.

Fr. Stephen J. Rossetti
I Am Awake

Precious Faith

■ **Trust the past to the mercy of God, the present to divine love, and the future to divine providence.** *St. Augustine*

May grace and peace be yours in abundance.

Blessed be the God and Father of our Lord Jesus Christ, who in his great mercy gave us a new birth to a living hope through the resurrection of Jesus Christ from the dead, to an inheritance that is imperishable, undefiled and unfading, kept in heaven for you who, by the power of God, are safeguarded through faith, to a salvation that is ready to be revealed in the final time. In this you rejoice, although now for a little while you may have to suffer through various trials, so that the genuineness of your faith, more precious than gold that is perishable even though tested by fire, may prove to be for praise, glory and honor at the revelation of Jesus Christ. Although you have not seen him you love him, you rejoice with an indescribable and glorious joy, as you attain the goal of your faith, the salvation of your souls.

1 Peter 1:2-9

Our House

■ **Anyone who hears my words is like the wise man who built his house on rock.** Matthew 7:24

Psychologists tell us that images of houses in our dreams are symbols of the inner self, the psyche. Can we learn to build the houses of our self-image upon the rock of God's love for us, or do we carefully construct them upon the shifting sands of other people's approval? God knows our innermost heart, our deepest darkness and still loves us with an infinite passion.

Nothing can shake that bond. Nothing can separate us, as St. Paul says, from the love of God. When we base our self-esteem on what others think of us or how much status, popularity, or reward we have, the ground is shaky indeed. On the other hand, if we can place our trust in God's love for us as our foundation, then we will not fear the changing winds of fame or fortune.

Denise Barker

Lord, when the house of my soul is buffeted by winds of flattery or scorn, teach me to come inside and to find comfort and guidance in the everlasting security of your care.

Human Dignity

■ **Give to the one who begs from you. Do not turn your back on the borrower.** Matthew 5:42

Human beings are to be valued for what they are, not for what they have. In loving the poor and serving those in whatever need, the Church seeks above all to respect and heal their human dignity. The aim of Christian solidarity and service is to defend and promote, in the name of Jesus Christ, the dignity and fundamental human rights of every person . . .

Institutions are very important and indispensable. But no institution can by itself replace the human heart, human compassion, human love or human initiative when dealing with the sufferings of another. This refers to physical sufferings, but it is even more true when we are in the many kinds of moral suffering and when the soul is suffering.

. . . Work against human ills must necessarily take into account the reality of creation and redemption. It means treating everyone as a unique child of God, a brother or sister of Jesus Christ. The path of human solidarity is the path of service, and true service means selfless love, open to the needs of all, without distinction.

Pope John Paul II
Homily, San Antonio, 9/13/'87

Suffering With Jesus

■ **We are constantly being given up to death for the sake of Jesus, so that the life of Jesus may be manifested in our mortal flesh.** 2 Corinthians 4:11

Suffering abounds in our world today and it is difficult and even impossible to know why God allows it, why some are so heavily burdened while others seem to get by unscathed.

It is only when we recall how God's Son accepted the chalice of suffering offered by his Father that suffering begins to become meaningful. We can identify with Jesus in his being rejected, betrayed, insulted, humiliated, mocked, scorned and, finally, subject to torture and a cruel death.

When we realize that the suffering and death of Jesus led to the glory of his resurrection and new life, our sufferings can be seen as the seed from which we receive not only new life, but the power to share this life with others.

Sr. Peter Dupreé

Lord, help me to accept suffering when it comes my way.

Precious Moments

■ **All of us, gazing on the Lord's glory with unveiled faces, are being transformed from glory to glory into his very image by the Lord who is the Spirit.**

2 Corinthians 3:18

If we were to record our moments of closeness to the Lord on a daily or weekly basis, we would find that these times of grace increase as we honor them with our attention. Many moments of nearness to Christ are lost because we are not watchful, our hearts closed.

To seek the Lord is to wake every morning with a humble anticipation of God's presence. We do not demand experiences of God, we are open to signs of divine movement in our daily life. It may happen in a coincidence, a dream, an embarass-ment. It may be in the face of a child, co-worker or stranger. It comes from our bodies, on the wind, in the earth and sky.

We can collect these moments and store them as treasures of the heart. As our treasure grows in size and variety, we begin to see that all things po-tentially are holy. The sacred is not separate, not a world apart. Holy moments are here and now for those who seek the Lord.

Nancy Summers

Lord, may I always be open to the precious moments of grace you give me in my daily life.

A Prayer For 'Enemies'

■ **But I say this to you: love your enemies . . .**

Matthew 5:44

Dear Lord, I hear your Gospel today tell us to love our enemies. I never seem to have too much trouble with this command, Lord, when I think about Hitler and Stalin and people like that. I find I can forgive them and even pray for them. It makes me feel free and noble to forgive a big-time enemy.

But I wonder if you meant something more by "Love your enemies." I have a feeling that you were speaking with your tongue in your cheek, and maybe we are misunderstanding you.

Does not your command also mean that we should be more loving toward those who make themselves obnoxious to us by getting on our nerves, upsetting our plans, making unreasonable demands? When people begin to do these things, I find myself regarding them as "temporary enemies." Lord, then the command to love my enemies becomes a real challenge, the more so because in loving and forgiving these "little enemies," there is nothing to boost my ego.

Dear Lord, send your Holy Spirit to open the eyes of my soul that I may not go through life blind to the truth of your words.

Sr. Mary Terese Donze, A.S.C.

Virtue Of Simplicity

■ **I myself am the living bread come down from heaven.** John 6:51

When we were preparing our children for first Eucharist, my husband and I began with a very basic question: "Why doesn't Jesus come to us in something more fancy like chocolate chip cookies or donuts?" The children wrestled with several possibilities ranging from the hazards posed by melting chocolate to the expense of the ingredients; eventually, however, we were able to steer them toward another consideration: "Because bread is simple stuff and is found all over the world."

Simple stuff, yes, but essential for life. Too often we look for more sophisticated foods with cholesterol-ridden sauces and French names; too often we settle for junk food because it is convenient. Both leave us empty and fail to nurture us. In identifying himself as the bread of life, Jesus points out that it is only in him that our hungers will be satisfied; in him alone will we find the rich food for which our hearts crave.

Elizabeth-Anne Vanek

Hopefulness

■ **Enough then of worrying about tomorrow.**

Matthew 6:34

We cannot live without hope. We have to have some purpose in life, some meaning to existence. We have to aspire to something. Without hope, we begin to die.

Why does it sometimes happen that a seemingly healthy person, successful in the eyes of the world, takes an overdose of sleeping pills and commits suicide? Why, on the other hand, do we see a seriously disabled person filled with great zest for life? Is it not because of hope? The one has lost all hope; in the other, hope is alive and overflowing. So hope does not stem from talents and gifts, or from health and success! It comes from something else. More precisely, hope comes from someone else, someone beyond ourselves.

Hope comes from God, from faith in God. People of hope are those who believe God created them for a purpose and that God will provide for their needs. They believe that God loves them as a faithful Father. Do you remember the advice that Jesus gave his disciples when they seemed to be fearful of the future? Stop worrying . . . Yes, God knows all our needs. God is . . . our hope.

Pope John Paul II
Homily, Los Angeles, 9/15/'87

Least Resistance

■ **Offer no resistance to injury.** Matthew 5:39

We grow more through rejection than acceptance, because acceptance breeds complacency while rejection brings awareness of the points in us that need correction. My only guru is the person who disturbs me, because he reveals my problem to me. **Rejoice, then, when a negative feeling has been aroused in you, because if you follow it up, it will lead you closer to liberation.** All growth occurs through suffering, if only you know how to use suffering to end suffering. Don't distract yourself from suffering, don't rationalize it, don't justify it, don't forget it, don't neglect it. The only way to deal with suffering is to face it, to observe it, to understand it.

Every time I suffer, I am resisting reality. Suffering is simply resistance to reality. I had obscured reality by my attachments, illusions and conditioning, and now reality, when it presents itself to me as it is and as I don't anymore know it, hurts me. The question to ask when suffering comes is, "What am I resisting?" Every time I am disturbed, there is something wrong with me. I am not prepared for what has come, I am out of tune with things.

Fr. Carlos G. Valles, S.J.
Mastering Sadhana

Called To Be Disciples

■ **How does that concern you? Your business is to follow me.** John 21:22

We fail. How many times! And we are, in the face of our many failures, tempted to become discouraged, to feel that we can never be true disciples of Christ. We begin to reconcile ourselves to being some kind of borderline Christian, one who will, by God's mercy, somehow slip into the outer reaches of heaven. Jesus heard the dying thief; we can hope he will hear us when we cry out from our deathbeds. But for us there is no hope of being a true disciple. We have all our passions and emotions. We are men and women of the world with family and business to preoccupy us . . . we can't leave all things to follow on the high adventure of discipleship.

Or can we?

. . . Peter was called. That is something important to remember. It was Jesus who chose Peter . . . and with all his faults and failures and human weakness, Peter followed. We too are called. And we too can follow, even with all our faults and failures and weaknesses.

Fr. M. Basil Pennington
Daily We Follow Him

The Beachcomber

■ **Keep your deeds of mercy secret, and your Father who sees in secret will repay you.** Matthew 6:4

A family of five were enjoying their day at the beach. The children were bathing in the ocean and making castles in the sand when in the distance a little old lady appeared. Her gray hair was blowing in the wind and her clothes were dirty and ragged. She was muttering something to herself as she picked up things from the beach and put them into a bag.

The parents called the children to their side and told them to stay away from the old lady. As she passed by, bending down every now and then to pick things up, she smiled at the family. But her greeting was not returned.

Many weeks later they learned that the little old lady had made it her lifelong crusade to pick up bits of glass from the beach so children wouldn't cut their feet.

Fr. Anthony de Mello, S.J.
Taking Flight

O Lord, I am so quick to judge others by outward appearances. Help me to see beyond the surface—and to appreciate what I see.

Trusting God

■ **Do not worry about tomorrow.** Matthew 6:34

Jesus tells us to trust God. It is not the message that we hear repeatedly in our society. Daily we are urged to trust ourselves and our money, to take care of all our needs and wants—not only now but for the future. Look at the vast array of insurance policies that cover people for every conceivable loss! Look at the vast assortment of annuities and financial plans that promise security against any future scarcity! Look at the popularity of state-run lotteries where the money prizes are obscenely large!

Does the race for financial security and protection result in people who are more psychologically secure, healthier and happier? Often not. People who seem to have gained financial security often worry just as much or more than they did before.

Jesus is not condemning prudence. And there are some situations in which even highly committed Christians probably find themselves worrying despite their best intentions. What we must do is remind ourselves daily that God loves us and cares for us, and that it is Godwe must depend on.

James E. Adams

Jesus, may I realize that my Father knows my needs and will give me the help I need.

A Prayer When Sinking

■ **Teacher, doesn't it matter to you that we are going to drown?** Mark 4:38

Several times I've almost drowned, Lord. Do you remember when I tried to walk on water and sank? I was six at the time and was visiting my cousins in Switzerland. If it hadn't been for that lame man's cane, I would have stayed at the bottom of Lake Geneva. And there was the time the glass fell out of my mask when I was snorkeling . . . and the time the waves carried me out to sea on an air mattress . . . and then last summer, when I got caught in the undertow.

There have been so many encounters with water, Lord. One could say that I have become expert in drowning. I know the tug and pull of currents, the roll of powerful waves, the helplessness of being tossed this way and that, like driftwood. But I have also known your embrace in the midst of storm. You snatched me from raging waters, calming my fears, giving me courage. You have set me on dry land, steadying my feet, gently leading me away from danger. In the midst of howling gales, I have heard you whisper, "Do not be afraid." For this I thank you, Lord, for this I praise you.

Elizabeth-Anne Vanek

Waiting In Silence

■ **At that moment, his mouth was opened and his tongue loosed, and he began to praise God.** Luke 1:64

If John the Baptist had been born years earlier as his parents had prayed, he could not have played his unique role in salvation. Their waiting, which seemed so fruitless, turned out to be a wait for the proper moment, for God's time. But a doubting Zechariah is struck dumb. After months in silence, Zechariah explodes in a beautiful song of praise (Luke 1:68-79).

How rich in inspiration for our daily living is this story! How often do we want things on our time, and, if we don't get them, we give up in bitterness? We just cannot wait. Yet often don't we see later that what we eventually got was better? We must wait for the right time, God's time—even as we realize that there may never come a "right time" for **all** we want.

And how often has either a startling good or sudden jolt of evil in life left us dumb? Speechless, because of joy or because of pain? Like Zechariah, we can use these experiences of forced silence and introversion to let the Word of God penetrate deeply into our hearts so that, when our voices return, we praise God.

James E. Adams

Lord, help me to wait in prayerful silence.

In the Dark

■ **As the sun was about to set, a trance fell upon Abram, and a deep, terrifying darkness enveloped him.** Genesis 15:12

How fitting that Abraham, "our father in faith," should have experienced the first "dark night of the soul"! God was about to establish a covenant with him, and Abraham had prepared the sacrifice just as he had been asked. Now it was God's turn to take over, and in order to witness that, Abraham had to be plunged into a "terrifying darkness."

Why? Not because God enjoys terrorizing those who are trying to live faithfully. Not because God is playing tricks or keeping secrets. But even great models of faith like Abraham must learn to grow in their faith, and that can happen only when God takes over. That is terrifying because it is beyond our control; it is darkness because it is beyond our understanding. Could Abraham ever have imagined so wonderful a covenant as God was about to make with him?

Mark Neilsen

Dear God, thank you for the example of Abraham, who believed and didn't run away in terror. May we who follow Jesus come to have such courage.

A Golden Goal

■ **Do to others whatever you would have them do to you. This is the law and the prophets.** Matthew 7:12

The famous "Golden Rule," carries more than one meaning. The usual interpretation is that we should be generous and fair in our dealings with other people. But if we pay close attention to Jesus' words, it is clear that in order to do this we must first be aware of the ways we like to be treated with fairness and generosity ourselves.

How would I like my children to talk to me? Quietly and with respect, and sometimes I like some kidding around. Is it possible, I ask myself, for me to raise my voice less often when communicating with my kids? Is this an impossible goal?

When I go into a supermarket, how would I like the clerk at the check-out stand to relate to me? With courtesy, and don't treat me like just another order to ring up and hurry through the check-out process. So, I should relate to the clerk as a unique individual, too, with courtesy and a kind word sincerely spoken.

The opportunities for putting the "Golden Rule" into effect are as countless as the stars in the sky.

Mitch Finley

Worthiness

■ **Put on then, as God's chosen ones, holy and beloved, heartfelt compassioin, kindness, humility, gentleness and patience, bearing with one another and forgiving one another.** Colossians 3:12-13

A basic temptation is the refusal to love those whom we consider, for some reason or other, unworthy of love. And, on top of that, to consider others unworthy of love for even very trivial reasons. Not that we hate them, of course. But we just refuse to accept them in our hearts, to treat them without suspicion and deal with them without inner reservations. In a word, we reject those who do not please us.

We are "charitable toward them." An interesting use of the word "charity" to cover and to justify a certain coldness, suspicion and even disdain.

We have to get along without constantly applying the yardstick of "worthiness" (who is worthy to be loved, and who is not). And it almost means, by implication, that we cease to ask even indirect questions about who is "justified," who is worthy of acceptance, who can be tolerated by the believer!

Thomas Merton
Conjectures of a Guilty Bystander

Be Prepared

■ **Prepare to meet your God, O Israel.** Amos 4:12

As much as our loving God wants us to live our life on earth to the fullest, we must also remember the warning to be prepared for death. Rather than this being the "first day of the rest of our lives," as the pop saying goes, perhaps we should think about being prepared if this would be our last day.

Would we be prepared? If we knew in advance when we were going to die, what special preparations would we make? Tell family and friends we love them? Pray more frequently? Make peace with enemies? Give money to charity? Receive the Sacrament of Reconciliation, go to Mass and Holy Communion? Wouldn't things like a child's spilling milk and a rude driver cutting us off in traffic seem insignificant on our last day on earth?

When we go through this exercise, don't we realize that we should live each day as if it were our last day on earth.

Joyce Miller

Jesus, help us live and love each day as if it were our last—not out of fear, but simply out of the wisdom that death gives us for our life here.

Keeping The Faith

■ **I have fought the good fight. I have finished the race. I have kept the faith. From now on a merited crown awaits me.** 2 Timothy 4:7-8

Go backward in time, and imagine yourself in your mother's womb. Enclosed within the womb, you can touch your mother with your feet, with your hands, with your whole body. You are aware of her, you feel and touch her, but you do not see her. The time for that has not yet come . . .But can you really have any doubts about her—her presence, her reality? Even though you cannot see her, you began life in your mother's womb, and in all beginnings there are things—many things—that must be accepted without understanding. Only faith and hope can throw any light on the beginning: faith, which is the eye of the reality you cannot see, and hope, which is the conviction that you will be born when it is time. In the beginning you have a thousand ways of experiencing the presence of the one who will bring you to birth, but you must accept your limitations, your own immaturity, inexorably bound up with the passage of time which does not belong to you and whose child you are.

Your moment will come! And when it does, you will emerge from the womb of time.

Carlo Carretto
In Search of the Beyond

God And Space

■ **The heavens proclaim your glory, O God, and the firmament shows forth the work of your hands.**

Psalm 19:1

We honor the Lord's intelligence and creative imagination insufficiently if we think that God has created billions of stars, millions of times larger than earth, only to twinkle far off and be our joy in the magic of the night or only for the pleasure of creating the most monumental ballet. Surely the Lord has sown life throughout these worlds of worlds—intelligent, free life, on our level, below it and above it.

When the real space landings have begun, men and women will at last be able to understand their littleness and greedy, cheap use that they have so often made of the gift of divine life, intelligence, and freedom in which they have been invited to share. They will at last be able to see how infinitely greater, how much more generous, how much better the Lord is than they have ever been able to imagine.

Dom Helder Camara
Questions for Living

Yearn For The Spirit

■ **You yourselves will not be the speakers; the Spirit of your Father will be speaking in you.** Matthew 10:20

To be filled with the Spirit, we must ask for the Spirit. But it is not enough to ask with our lips. We have to empty ourselves of our self-sufficiency if we are to receive the Holy Spirit. We have to empty ourselves of all our idols if we are to have room for the true God with us. We have to be like the apostles in the upper room, aware of our nothingness so that God the creator can make something out of nothing.

To experience the Spirit, we must yearn for the Spirit. We must seek it, desire it, long for it. We must make ourselves ready to receive God's gift by asking for it not only with our mind but with our heart and our gut. Jesus said, "Ask and you will receive," but if we do not really ask, how can we ever really receive?

When we have done all that, all we can do is let God love us, let God give grace to us, let God be gracious to us, let God shower gifts on us. **If we wait in patient expectation, the Lord will come. If we do not try to be worthy, the Spirit will be given.** If we trust in God's promise, we will not be disappointed.

Fr. Richard Rohr, O.F.M. & Joseph Martos
The Great Themes of Scripture:New Testament

The Highest Truth

■ **You have forgiven the guilt of your people; you have covered all their sins.** Psalm 85:3

God wants all of us to grow in knowledge of divine love. In this pursuit, guilt is of no help at all.

God is love. That is the most important truth we can ever learn. Christ taught it by his life and example. He knew his Father's love. He taught his followers that this love touched them as well.

An upright life is beautiful, but it is a struggle. **Today, any discussion of guilt as a blessing and a source of strength, valid though it is, needs to be balanced by the truth of God's unchanging love.** We can use guilt as a signal, an interior impetus to move on to something higher and better, but it should never obliterate the truth that God loves all of us, even the most hardened criminal, with an infinite love.

Fr. John Catoir
Enjoy the Lord

O God, may I never be so preoccupied with my sins and my guilt that I forget to keep your infinite love for me always in my mind and heart.

Thorny Reminders

■ **That I might not become conceited I was given a thorn in the flesh, an angel of Satan to beat me.**

2 Corinthians 12:7

When I was a boy, I looked on the Church as separate from the world. Now I see the Church quite differently because I have learned to see myself differently. The hotchpotch of good and bad, greatness and wretchedness, sanctity and sin, is, at bottom, **me. In me there is everything.** In me lives the world and the Church. In me there is capacity for evil and yearning for holiness, corrupt nature and sanctifying grace. In me there is Adam and there is Christ . . .

I must not present myself to sinners as holy, to the unjust as just, to the impure as pure. I must be careful not to be too hasty in climbing on to my soap box and preaching to others . . .

I ought to be more humble in my attitude. I must be not so ready to judge others as vessels of the world's sin and feel myself to be the ever-innocent because I belong to the Church.

Carlo Carretto
I Sought and I Found

O God, may pain and weakness not break my back but may it bend my knee.

Still Waters

■ **Without warning a violent storm came up on the lake, and the boat began to be swamped by the waves. Jesus was sleeping soundly, so they made their way to him and woke him: "Lord, save us! We are lost."**

Matthew 8:24-25

When in danger, when in doubt,
Run in circles, scream and shout!

This old rhyme is not advice; it's a description of what we generally do when we are fearful and confused. We know it's futile, but we do it anyway!

This tendency is addressed in the British navy by a custom known as "the still." In cases of sudden disaster aboard ship, the call for "the still" is blown. This is a whistle for the crew to come to complete silence. When "the still" is blown every sailor aboard knows what it means—prepare to do the right thing. This moment of calm has helped avoid many a catastrophe that "running in circles, screaming and shouting" could cause . . .

When the storms come, we need to seek out Jesus, to find a deep, calming presence of peace within the center of our life . . . we need the serenity that comes from God as we surrender our doubts and fears into the divine hands.

A. Philip Parham
Letting God

A Myth Of The Good Self

■ **He who seeks only himself brings himself to ruin, whereas he who brings himself to naught for me discovers who he is.** Matthew 10:39

The cultural myth is that in self-control, self-determination, self-direction, self-identity and self-confidence lies the good life. Nearly every cultural institution reflects this belief . . . psychotherapy, politics, education. All are children of the same craziness, the insanity which says self-determination is utopia . . .

Even religion, the great timeless gate to beyond-the-self, becomes a technique. A means to an end for self-improvement. To create better behavior, to make more abiding happiness, to manufacture holiness. There are times when, through religion, one comes close to turning over self-control. Offering it up. Giving up. Sacrificing the delusion. But even then, most often, it becomes the turning over of a defective self to the ultimate fixer in the sky, in the hopes of getting a rebuilt and perfected self in return. This is not going beyond self, nor is it giving up. It's using God to help one get back in control.

Gerald May
Simply Sane

Sin And Sickness

■ **When Jesus saw their faith he said to the paralytic, "Have courage, son, your sins are forgiven."**

Matthew 9:2

In this healing lies the central message of Jesus because he forges words to action in challenging the ancient belief that sin was the dark seed to which every illness could surely be traced.

Illness and disfigurement abounded in the ancient world, and so, the crippled and deformed could only be understood—could only be put in place theologically—if the sores, the dead staring eyes, and the shriveled limbs were the bitter fruit of the sinful lives of their predecessors . . . Postmodern people have not settled the issue. **Are we sick because we sin? Or do we sin because we are sick?** Can sin be boiled down to a sliver of psychiatric residue in our souls? We remain unsure of the answers . . .

The rabbis of Jesus' time had written of the need for forgiveness of sin before a cure of illness could be expected. It was a staple of their religious outlook, and in it, of course, only God could forgive sins. So Jesus by this action speaks a new religious language; he acts as only God can by declaring that the paralytic's sins are forgiven, that he can arise and walk.

Eugene Kennedy
The Choice to be Human

One Of A Kind

■ **I drew them with human cords, with bands of love; I fostered them like one who raises an infant to his cheeks.** Hosea 11:4

God did not want a world without you or me, because of his special predilection and love for us . . . God also could have chosen a world . . . with a different you and a different me. But God did not want a different you. It is this you that God loves, the you with your actual fingerprints, hair color, voice and heart, with your unique and unrepeatable immortal soul.

God does not love us as one big glob of humanity. God loves each of us individually. There is no one and there will never be anyone like each of us. Our lives, and the other individual circumstances and personal determinations of those lives, are God's special gift. Divine providence has chosen and destined you and me, by a special act of love, to deliver a message, to sing a song, and to confer an act of love on this world which no one else can. Each of us is a unique and unrepeatable image and likeness of God, a unique and unrepeatable mystery of God's love. You and I have been known and loved by God from all eternity and through all eternity.

Fr. John Powell, S.J.
Through Seasons of the Heart

All Need Reform

■ **I have come to call not the self-righteous, but sinners.** Matthew 9:13

These words contain a great comfort to all sinners, but they also offer a challenge. Jesus is speaking to the Pharisees, people too ready to judge others and ignore their own sins. The Pharisees knew they were not perfect, but they had become accustomed to their sins. Perhaps they found a way to excuse themselves while they gave no "benefit of the doubt" to anyone else.

Are there some sins we're willing to overlook while others we regard as inexcusable? Do we condemn one group of sinners but are blind to the faults of another?

That isn't Jesus' way. Instead, he invites everyone to reform and is scornful of those who believe themselves justified by their own actions. If we are willing to reform or to become aware of our need to reform, Jesus will be there for us.

Mark Neilsen

God, help me to pray this ancient prayer with all my heart: "Lord Jesus Christ, Son of God, have mercy on me, a sinner."

Helping Jesus Heal

■ **Jesus stood up and followed him.** Matthew 9:19

Matthew's account of a synagogue leader who asks Jesus to restore his fallen daughter is a telling episode about prayer. When the man asks Jesus for help, the next verse reports that "Jesus stood up and followed him." Jesus was immediately obedient to the supplication, but Jesus did not rush on ahead—he followed the petitioner.

When we go to Jesus with our requests, are we leading the way? Jesus will follow us to our place of need. Jesus does not leave us behind and answer our prayer without us. So if we are praying for a sick and lonely aunt, we must first go to her ourselves (or at least send a card), knowing Jesus is following us to provide us with the graces to help us care for that aunt. It is all too easy in prayer to try to turn our responsibilities over to Jesus and then walk away. Our prayers of petition are not complete until we personally lead Jesus, insofar as we are able, to the situation.

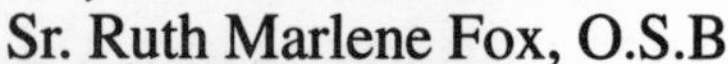

Sr. Ruth Marlene Fox, O.S.B

Being Prepared

■ **He told them to take nothing on the journey.**
Mark 6:8

Jesus told his disciples to carry with them in their ministry only sandals and a walking stick. No food, no money, no traveling bag. No granola bars or juice for quick energy on the road. No portable radios, inspirational books or pads of scratch paper. No sweaters for cold nights or shorts and T-shirts for hot days. No first aid kits, no Chap Stick, maps, travelers checks, insurance cards or list of emergency numbers. In a word, simply themselves is all they are to take.

Few of us would embark on a journey without "being prepared." We know instinctively what items will give us greater comfort and security. On our spiritual journeys, however, "being prepared" means abandoning our props and supports, and entrusting ourselves to God. It means learning detachment from things, places and even people, so that we have the freedom we need to see and love God. Whether we soar with God or walk with God, any luggage, however small, may work to pull us down.

Elizabeth-Anne Vanek

Jesus, help me to learn to "travel light" in my spiritual journey.

Peak Experiences

■ **He who loses his life for my sake will find it.**

Matthew 10:39

St. Benedict called a monastery a workshop and a school . . . for the pursuit . . . of heightened awareness . . . of sensitivity to peak experiences that can come to us at any time if we are truly present in the now.

What is a peak experience? Maybe for you it was a moment on a mountaintop. Maybe it was a passage in a book, a poem, or a melody. Or sitting on a fence rail dangling your legs in utter absorption . . . What makes the peak experience so liberating is that precisely for once I no longer feel that I feel and know that I know but simply feel and know and just that. Only afterward can I reflect on it and so talk about it. And what I am then inclined to say is something like "I was simply swept off my feet." Or "I had lost myself." This is all. But not quite all. For looking back I will so admit that at the moment of my peak experience I was more truly and more fully myself than at any other time. And so I find myself confronted with **the strange paradox that I am most truly myself when I forget myself.** When I lose myself, I find my Self.

Br. David Steindl-Rast, O.S.B.
A Listening Heart

O Lord, Comfort Me

■ **May our Lord Jesus Christ himself and God our Father, who has loved us and given us everlasting encouragement and good hope through his grace, encourage your hearts and strengthen them in every good deed and word.** 2 Thessalonians 2:16-17

O my God, let me never forget that seasons of consolation are refreshments here, and nothing more—they are not our abiding state. They will not remain with us, except in heaven. Here they are only intended to prepare us for action and for suffering.

I pray you, O my God, to give them to me from time to time. Shed over me the sweetness of your presence, lest I faint by the way; lest I find religious service wearisome, through my exceeding infirmity, and give up prayer and meditation; lest I go about my daily work in a dry spirit, or am tempted to take pleasure in it for its own sake, and not for you.

Give me your divine consolations from time to time; but let me not rest in them. Let me use them for the purpose for which you give them. Let me not think it terrible, let me not be downcast, if they go. Let them carry me forward to the thought and desire of heaven.

John Henry Newman
Prayers, Poems, Meditations

Trust Divine Providence

■ **I am your brother Joseph, whom you once sold into Egypt. But now do not be distressed, and do not reproach yourselves for having sold me here. It was really for the sake of saving lives that God sent me here ahead of you . . . Even though you meant harm to me, God meant it for good.** Genesis 45:4-5; 50:20

Conscience has to be heeded, and public morality to be respected. But we just don't know what is good and what is bad for anybody, and that, in the midst of our humble limitations, should give us great peace when making decisions. We are not burdened now with the responsibility to solve all problems for everybody and to ensure the universal welfare of humankind.

It is for us only, in the honesty of our conscience and within the boundaries of our actions, to approximate results, and God is the one who will change the bad luck we have one day into good luck the next day through divine providence. If we only understood this, the burden of our moral conscience would be considerably lightened.

Fr. Carlos G. Valles, S.J.
Mastering Sadhana

Mystery And Meaning

■ **Nothing is concealed that will not be revealed, and nothing hidden that will not become known.**

Matthew 10:26

One thing is certain: we are on earth as in a huge space where everything is light and dark at the same time, where everything is the sign of an invisible presence, and where a continual challenge comes from the splendid vault outstretched above in its astronomical distances.

Inaccessible far-away things question us endlessly, oblige us to look up at those luminous specks like starry holes piercing the black vault, which seem to say that there, above, is the repose we seek.

How often, lying wrapped in a blanket on the sand, have I passed hour after hour gazing at a starry dome ceaselessly speaking to me, questioning me, helping me to find my bearings in the dark! Why do we live? Why do things come to be? Why do I plod along like a wandering shepherd? Why this vast silence? Why do stars look down as though indifferent to our suffering?

Withal, one thing is certain: this light, the sign of truth we seek and the means by which we may catch a glimpse of it, has not got its roots on earth.

Carlo Carretto
Why O Lord?

Godly Mercy

■ **It is mercy I desire and not sacrifice.** Matthew 12:7

The saints remind us that God wants and expects us to have mercy on others. We are to build others up rather than tear them down. Maybe they need tough love, but that does not give us license to use the clenched fist of anger or the whip of revenge. Everyone has a claim on our mercy, strangers as well as loved ones. No one exists who does not need mercy. We are all weak, and the strength we do have can vanish in a blink.

There is a sense in which we need to have mercy on ourselves as well by not being too hard on ourselves for our failings. And we need to realize that we don't have mercy on others because we think we are better than they. That "mercy" is arrogance. **Rather, we have mercy because we identify with others, we see how much we are alike.** We see them as fellow pilgrims, as brothers and sisters.

As we treat others, so we will be treated. What a blessing it will be when we fall and need mercy if we have been merciful to others. For we can confidently look for God's mercy.

Fr. Bernard Schumacher, O.S.B.

O God, may my motivation for mercy stem from the fact that I truly see others as my brothers and sisters!

Earth Watch

■ **Christ Jesus is the image of the invisible God, the first-born of all creatures. In him everything in heaven and on earth was created.** Colossians 1:15-16

In the eyes of faith the earth is not a limitless, exploitable reservoir, but a part of the mystery of creation, which one may not treat greedily, but rather which we owe wonder and reverence.

To arrive at this attitude, we need a culture of asceticism which will enable people and the diverse human communities to achieve freedom also as a readiness to renounce one's own power and greatness, and thus from within themselves make room for others, particularly the weak. Making room like this is an aspect of love for people, but also for God.

It is not too late for a radical conversion to the person in harmony with others, to the earth as a living space which is meant to be a garden and must not become a desert, even if the believer does not see it as a lasting homeland. It is not too late to turn to God, who already searches for us.

Pope John Paul II
Speech in Salzburg, 6/26/'88

The Art Of Selflessness

■ **Whoever finds his life will lose it, while whoever loses his life for my sake will find it.** Matthew 10:39

Whenever and wherever you encounter yourself, an image of self, an evaluation of self, a fear of self, a desire for self, self-consciousness, pride or guilt or whatever, don't kill it. There is no need for battle. One needs do nothing special with it. Just back off from it a little, see it and take a deep breath. Let it be and its energy will, in time, be free . . . Let your self be. Totally. Without a single iota of equivocation. Let it all exist, as awful or wonderful as it may seem. Permit it absolutely. If there is a desire to kill something, ask, "Who is killing whom?" And be exceedingly gentle. To struggle with yourself will make you very important.

Self-importance is a trap, but it is not something one can attack directly. If one makes a frontal attack on self-importance, success or failure will foster pride or guilt. These will make the self even *more* important. So it is foolish to try to stop being interested in one's self. It is much wiser to nurture interest in other realities. In awareness of the present. In whatever work needs to be done. In the sun and the wind. In other people.

Gerald May
Simply Sane

The Voices Of God

■ **There are differing workings but it is the same God who produces all of them in everyone. To each individual the manifestation of the Spirit is given for some benefit.** 1 Corinthians 12:6-7

Can God put a new idea directly and immediately into my *mind*? Can God give me a new perspective in which to view my life with its successes and failures, agonies and ecstasies? Can God put new desires into my *heart*, new strength into my *will*? Can God touch and calm my turbulent *emotions*? Can God actually whisper words to the listening ears of my soul through the inner faculty of my *imagination*? Can God stimulate certain *memories* stored within the human brain at the time these memories are needed? I feel sure that God can and does reach us in these ways.

I pray by telling God who I am and by listening to him as he reveals to me not only who he is, but also who I am, and what my life and this world mean to him. My listening to God is the silent turning over to him the five faculties or powers of perception through which I truly believe that he comes to me.

Fr. John Powell, S.J.
Through Seasons of the Heart

Joyful Repentance

■ **Yahweh . . . you take your people's guilt away.**
Psalm 85:2-3

An abiding sorrow for sin is a great grace. The saints had it, and that added a touch of humble sweetness to whatever they did. But to harbor feelings of uneasiness about our forgiven sins, to keep feeling guilty and unworthy in a way that makes us shy away from God, is not true sorrow for sin, and it deprives us of the joy God wants us to have in our repentance.

In repentance, we must rush back in childlike trust to God. St. Therese of Lisieux said that if her soul were burdened with countless mortal sins, she would throw herself into the arms of God and trust that all her wickedness would be forgiven—not because she deserved it, but because God is so good.

Recall the prodigal son, who was restored to his family without a word of reproach from his father. God is like that father. Let us be trusting children.

Sr. Mary Terese Donze, A.S.C.

Lord, help me to celebrate your forgiveness rather than brood over my sins & weaknesses.

Divine Origins

■ **Before I formed you in the womb, I knew you.**
Jeremiah 1:5

With billions of people on earth, can God really have a personal concern for each? For me, the individual that I am, living in this house, on this street, with these problems, these worries?

When you have such doubts that is a good time to read with humble and loving faith these words from the prophet Jeremiah. Those awesome, wonderful thrilling words are for each of us!

Think of God, eons ago, contemplating you, seeing you from all possible angles, analyzing the best time for you to appear on the earth so that you would meet certain other people who would count in your life—and theirs. See God looking about to choose your parents, setting up the genes and the physical conditions that would determine your five-foot-eight-inch height, your blonde hair, your blue eyes. God knowing you body and soul, inside and out.

God has invested too much in each of us to forget us.

Sr. Mary Terese Donze, A.S.C

My God, help me understand and appreciate the awesome fact that you have been thinking of me forever!

A Close Friend

■ **How precious is your kindness, O God!** Psalm 36:8

To have a friend who is always with you is such a blessing! That is what our faith tells us we have—a loving God who stands with us. And we are doubly blessed when we can feel the life-giving kindness of that God who is always available.

Our faith assures us of God's indwelling, assures us that God is with us, that God is open to us at any moment and in any place with divine healing, love and peace. We do not have to wait for a favorable time. We do not need an appointment or need to prepare what we want to say. We need only turn to the best of our ability to God, and the more we turn the more we become aware of God guiding and leading us through life. As our relationship with God deepens, the more conscious we will be of our Creator and Sustainer speaking lovingly to us in every facet of our lives.

Sr. Peter Dupreé

O God, help me to see and to feel what my faith assures me of—that I am always in your loving presence.

Mary Magdalene's Witness

■ **Jesus said to her, "Mary!" She turned to him and said [in Aramaic], "Rabbouni!" which means "Teacher."** John 20:16

Mary Magdalene, what is it like to be loved by God and to love God wholly in return?

First, it is recognizing your faults and failings and yet knowing that in spite of them, you are priceless and special. It is having the courage to open yourself up to relationships, to share, to love, to grow, realizing all the while you can be hurt. But the possibility of being hurt doesn't matter because, deep down, **you are secure that God will be there in the hurt, loving you, supporting you, helping you get through, bringing you to wholeness.**

Yet a love relationship with God is not all sweetness. The deeper your love grows, the more your eyes are opened to the world's pain and suffering. You reach out to love, to heal, but soon learn it cannot happen without the other person's willingness to be loved and healed. So you wait patiently as God waits for you.

It is not easy. But then there is your lover, calling your name in that special way and all the struggles and sacrifices are forgotten. What joy! God loves you.

Charlotte Rancilio

A Concrete Lesson

■ **Let us love one another, for love is of God.**

1 John 4:7

A psychology professor who had no children would often scold his neighbors for spanking their children. "You should love your kids, not punish them." One day the professor put in a new cement walk. He worked long hours trowelling and making it perfect. Just as he was finishing, he saw a little boy making handprints and writing in the cement. He rushed over, grabbed the boy and started to spank him. A neighbor leaned out the window and shouted, "Watch it, professor! Don't you remember? You must love the child." The professor yelled back, "I love him in the abstract but not in the concrete!"

Someone recently said, "We have a lot of love-talk but little love-action." Love is not love when it does not act. Love is only love when it is done, not just felt or talked about. "Love" is an active verb—and it demands "concrete" expression with deeds of love. Love can be demonstrated without words. The gift of love always is delivered by actual gifts and giving.

A. Philip Parham
Letting God

Learning To Share

■ **"Not even with two hundred days' wages could we buy loaves enough!"** John 6:7

Can we identify with the Apostles in this story of the loaves and fishes? Can we feel their frustration and inadequacy? Jesus seems to be asking them to do the impossible—to feed so large a crowd with so little food. (In Matthew's account, Jesus first says, "**You** feed them." Mt. 14:16)

We have material possessions and knowledge. We have skills and talents. Yet at times we may be pushed to do the impossible. The demands of family, job, community and world crowd in on us. There are so many hungers. What can we do with our limited resources?

The disciples simply stated their need to Jesus. After blessing their meager resources, Jesus handed the responsibility back to the disciples. After they shared, they had enough, with 12 baskets to boot!

We also can feel helpless when faced with the demands of human hunger. But the miracle of multiplication can happen many times if we also present the need to Jesus, allow him to bless us and our efforts—and then **do our part, which is sharing generously.** Many will be fed, more than we could imagine.

Sr. Ancilla Keinberger, O.P.

Accepting Our Limits

■ **We hold this treasure in earthen vessels, that the surpassing power may be of God and not from us. We are afflicted in every way, but not constrained; perplexed, but not driven to despair; persecuted, but not abandoned; struck down, but not destroyed; always carrying about in the body the dying of Jesus, so that the life of Jesus may also be manifested in our body.**

2 Corinthians 4:7-10

I need only seek truth, as I am personally called to do in my own situation. If I were more a man of love and spirit, more a man of God, I would have no problems. So my job is to advance with the difficulty of one who lacks love and yet seeks it, in the realization that I am not supposed to solve all my problems for myself. Nor am I supposed to be a man of God in the sense of "having no problem." **One of the sources of futile struggle in the spiritual life is the assumption that one has to become a person without problems,** which is, of course, impossible. And if people are struggling to be without problems in their lives, they are beating their heads against a brick wall.

Thomas Merton
A Vow of Conversation

Asking And Receiving

■ **God said, "Ask something of me and I will give it to you."** 1 Kings 3:5

The first thing for which I ever asked God was a shiny red cardboard suitcase to carry my books to school. I did have a leather satchel, but at six years old, one is conscious of what other children like: red cardboard was in, dull leather was out. I remember praying through the night that my mother would see the necessity of the purchase. The next day, I was the proud owner of one rather cheap, garish-but-just-like-everyone-else's suitcase. I congratulated myself upon my ability to pray and determined to do so more often.

At six years old, I was convinced that God had been actively involved in my new acquisition. Some thirty years later, I no longer imagine I can bend God so easily to my will. I no longer see prayer as the way "to get things," but as the experience of God's presence, a gift in itself. **I have come to understand that it is when I bend my will to God's that I receive what I ask for.** My accompanying delight has its source more in this union of wills than in what I receive.

Elizabeth-Anne Vanek

Anxious Moments

■ **The seed sown among the thorns is the one who hears the word, but then worldly anxiety and the lure of riches choke the word and it bears no fruit.**

Matthew 13:22

On those all-too-infrequent occasions when I am honest with myself, I realize that "worldly anxiety and the lure of riches" have long been "thorns in my side." They are noisy, clamorous, never-relenting parts of me that constantly shout out for my attention and time. I do not have to stop, or even slow down, in order to hear them. They are my weaknesses, to be sure, my Achilles' heal, my soft spot where the power of evil knows to aim.

But when I take the time to be quiet, to slow down my life, I hear a still, soft voice inside me that lures me to something higher and holier. It is a voice that does not clamor for attention. Yet it is persistent, always there when I care to listen. Only when I heed the Lord's command to "Be still and know that I am God" do I begin to hear the Word and bear fruit.

Steve Givens

The Good And Bad

■ The reign of God is also like a dragnet thrown into the lake, which collected all sorts of things.

Matthew 13:47

How much we want life (and religion as well) to be either one thing or another. To be either black or white. No shades. No mix of good and bad. The fact that everything and everybody is a mixture of good and bad makes it all so messy—much like a fish net writhing with all kinds of icky creatures.

The great dragnet that Jesus talks about does not discriminate, but contains "all sorts of things," good and bad and mediocre, sorrow and joy and boredom. We want only good fish in the net of life. No electric eels. No sting rays. No octopi. No sharks. No other undesirables. But Jesus says that only at the end is the sorting out—and that by God and the angels, not by us.

This metaphor forces me to ask, Do I look on the universe too moralistically? Do I accept as good only what conforms to my narrow definition? Do I act as if "evil" can be abolished once and for all and "good" enthroned forever? To live in God's often curious and frighteningly diverse world requires compassion and patience and joy. Those are the "dragnet" virtues.

James E. Adams

On The Rise

■ **The reign of God is like yeast which a woman took and kneaded into three measures of flour. Eventually the whole mass of dough began to rise.** Matthew 13:33

Because I make bread so infrequently, I am never quite sure whether or not the yeast I have on hand is any good. If it's not, the mass of dough will go nowhere; if it is, a marvelous transformation will happen and bread will be possible.

There are times that my spirits seem like a lump of dough that is incapable of any kind of movement. Flour, water and a little salt may be good for making paste, but it is hardly appetizing. Add some yeast and you've got something. When I feel about as spiritually dynamic as a mound of dough, sooner or later God's reign comes along to transform everything.

Like yeast itself, the reign of God is an everyday reality, yet always wonderful. Our "daily bread" is always being provided.

Mark Neilsen

Daily Revelations

■ **For in truth it was the Lord who sent me to you, to speak all these things for you to hear.** Jeremiah 26:15

If we only have ears to hear, God is speaking to us in all the events of our lives and not merely in times of formal prayer. Busy people will often say that their work is their prayer—a tricky slogan but one that contains an important grain of truth. It is true that everything that happens, everything that we do, is a revelation of God to us. But not every revelation by God is a genuine encounter for us.

How often have we had the experience of speaking to someone else and not being heard? We are speaking, revealing ourselves, but the other person is either not listening or is misunderstanding us. **The art of listening is at the heart of genuine prayer.** As we learn to listen with attention and sensitivity, all the events of our lives become encounters with the Lord, all events become prayer.

Fr. Thomas H. Green, S.J.
Opening to God

Silence Is Golden

■ **Be silent before the Lord God.** Zephaniah 1:7

We need silence. We need to be alone or together looking for God in silence. There it is that we accumulate the inward power by which we act, by which we do the smallest duty and by which we suffer the severest hardships that befall us.

Silence came before creation, and the heavens were spread without a word.

Christ was born in the dead of night; and though there has been no power like his, "He did not strive nor cry, neither was his voice heard in the streets."

Once I was asked by someone what I consider the most important aspect of the training of the sisters in our order. I answered: Silence. Interior and exterior silence. Silence is essential in a religious house. The silence of humility, of charity, the silence of the eyes, of the ears, of the tongue. There is no life of prayer without silence.

Silence, and then kindness, charity; silence leads to charity, and charity to humility.

Mother Teresa
My Life For The Poor

Dear God, give me the grace to keep a period of silence each day so that I may better hear your words and act on them.

Forgive And Forget

■ Peter came up to Jesus and asked him, "Lord, when my brother wrongs me, how often must I forgive him? Seven times?" "No," Jesus replied, "not seven times; I say, seventy times seven times." Matthew 18:21-22

People often fail to make a simple but important distinction between forgiveness as act, and forgiveness as feeling. If we don't distinghish, we find ourselves in an apparent dilemma.

The act of forgiveness is just that: **an act**, a choice, a decision based on our Christian convictions. It is an act of the will and intellect, based on our reasonableness. It's a reaching out to a person, inviting him or her back into a former relationship. It can be a difficult act but a firm one; it can be cold and devoid of accompanying warm, positive feelings, but nonetheless genuine. I suggest that Christ's act of forgiveness on the cross, "Father, forgive them for they know not what they are doing" might have been like this.

The **act** of forgiveness can be a fact but the **feeling** of forgiveness may come only in time. When we confront these "unforgiving feelings," deal with them honestly, and work through them, then they will gradually dissipate.

Fr. Martin H. Padovani
Healing Wounded Emotions

Masquerade

■ **Whenever Moses entered the presence of the Lord to converse with him, he removed the veil until he came out again.** Exodus 34:34

We often wear veils or masks in our relationships with others. Sometimes it is out of politeness. To be too frank can be not only rude, but disruptive. But sometimes our veil or mask hides our true selves from others. In doing that our true selves are often hidden from us as well. **We are in the dangerous position of not knowing what we truly feel.**

With God there is no need for masks or veils. Any pretense with God is useless and foolish. God has known us from the beginning of time and accepts us as we are. How refreshing it can be to turn to God and bare our hearts and minds and souls. Here is a friend who will never be bored or impatient. One who will not flatter or deceive, but will listen to all our petitions, all our concerns.

We pray to get closer to God, but open-hearted prayer also brings us closer to our true selves as well.

Joan Zrilich

Recognizing God's Help

■ **Happy are those whose strength is in you; they have courage to make the pilgrimage . . . Yahweh Sabaoth, happy are those who put their trust in you.**

Psalm 84:6, 13

A story is told about a man whose faith was considered very strong. When a river dam broke in a flood near the town where the man lived, the police came to evacuate homeowners. But the man refused to leave his home, saying the Lord would save him.

When the water forced the man to the second floor of his home, somebody came in a boat and offered to take him to safety. Again he refused, saying the Lord would save him. Finally, when the man was forced to the roof, a helicopter came to take him. But again he refused to leave. He soon drowned.

When he met the Lord, the man asked, "Why didn't you help me, Lord? I was counting on you." The Lord said, "I did offer help. First, I sent the police, then a boat and finally a helicopter."

Joyce Miller

O Lord, may I always be willing to recognize and accept the help I am sent.

Happy Endings

■ **You are not judging by God's standards, but by human standards.** Matthew 16:23

During the Great Depression, when the outlook for people was bleak, Hollywood began producing many movies based on the theme of going from rags to riches. And every movie had a happy ending . . .

In today's Gospel reading, Peter acknowledged that Jesus was the messiah, the son of the living God. But Peter failed to understand . . . he wanted a happy ending for Jesus and he could not see what death had to do with that. He did not understand the grand plan of God that Jesus would go from "rags to riches," from death to life. Jesus passed through the poverty of death to the riches of everlasting life. In dying he was not leaving us in the lurch. Rather he came into riches which he is more than eager to share with us through an eternal union of love, the new covenant.

Everybody loves a happy ending, even God. We must have the faith that God will lead us through all the difficulties and disappointments of this life to an eternal embrace when Jesus Christ comes again in glory to claim us as his own.

Fr. Charles E. Miller, C.M.
Opening the Treasures

The Fear Of Surrendering

■ **Unless a grain of wheat falls into the earth and dies, it remains by itself alone; but if it dies, it bears much fruit.** John 12:24

To surrender is to give over to God, to give up our power over something that keeps us down or holds us back. When we surrender, we open ourselves up to the mystery of life, to the risks of the future, to the challenge of the unknown.

For many of us it is scary to think of surrendering ourselves into the arms of God. "What might happen?" is the secret question that pummels our thoughts. We do not yet fully believe that God is always—yes, *always*—desiring our good and our happiness. **We do not yet fully realize that God will be with us as a guiding power to love and to sustain us through whatever hardships and heartaches life may bring.**

To surrender is to live with a mind and heart that is open to the future and to trust that all shall be well. When we let go and when we surrender, we are most surely on the pathway to healing.

Sr. Joyce Rupp, O.S.M.
Praying Our Goodbyes

'Attitude Of Gratitude'

■ **Give thanks to the Lord, acclaim his name; among the nations make known his deeds.** Isaiah 12:4

The story is told of a man sitting on a crowded subway reading his paper. He noticed an elderly woman standing above him, stood up, tipped his hat, and offered her his seat. The woman dropped her packages, her eyes widened, and then suddenly closed as she fainted on the spot. When she was revived, she looked up into the face of the kind man who had offered his seat and said, "Thank you."

Then the man fainted.

A philosopher once said, "God has two dwellings; one in heaven and the other in a thankful heart." If there is any one element essential to (a genuine Christian life), it is "an attitude of gratitude."

A. Philip Parham
Letting God

God has two dwellings; one in heaven and the other in a thankful heart.

Celebration Time

■ **He dispatched his servants to summon the invited guests to the feast, but they refused to come.**

Matthew 22:3

Is it a Christian virtue to be grim? Jesus compares the kingdom of heaven to a wedding feast, and we act much of the time like we're on our way to a funeral. We are, of course, on our way to a funeral—our own. But that fact changes nothing as far as Jesus is concerned. Put on, he cries, the wedding garment of good deeds. Then, come in! Dance! Eat! Celebrate!

Not worthy, you say? Sorry, my friend, but that is irrelevant. "The servants went out into the streets and gathered all they found, bad and good alike, and the hall was filled with guests" (Matthew 22:10). The compassion and forgiveness of God have no end, as long as we are willing to accept.

What it comes down to is this: are we willing to respond to God's invitation to come to the wedding feast, even now? Or do we insist on staying out in the cold? Do we refuse even to believe that God would invite us to such a wedding feast?

Mitch Finley

My Gifts To Share

■ **"We have nothing here but five loaves and a couple of fish."** Matthew 14:17

You have already equipped me, Lord, with all I need to meet whatever challenges this day holds for me. As the day unfolds, keep me from slipping into the "if-only" mindset. If only I had **her** patience. If only I had **his** wisdom. If only I had this talent or that. Precious time is wasted in adding these to my many petitions.

I take myself and my gifts so much for granted. A deeper look inside will help me to discover, to uncover what is uniquely mine to give. Whatever it may be, I know that before this day is over I will be called upon to share it with another. **I must be ready and waiting to share my gifts.**

And if all I find within are five loaves and a couple of fish? All I need do is give my seemingly insignificant gifts to you, O Lord, and watch you transform them right before my eyes, for the good of all.

Sr. Mary Charleen Hug, S.N.D.

Do I have a genuine respect for myself and my gifts? Do I try always to compare myself to others? Do I fail to share my gifts because I underrate them?

Reaching Out

■ **Not a single one of these little ones shall ever come to grief.** Matthew 18:14

Jesus' compassion for the little ones and lost sheep is strikingly clear. We need to hear it just as much as the people of his time, this compassion for lepers and Gentiles, Samaritans and sinners. Things have not really changed that much.

Our world is filled with the unprotected, the lost, the small ones who have no power or resources and are totally dependent. They are the homeless, the physically and mentally handicapped, the unwed mothers. The list goes on. **Who are the small ones in our immediate world?** There may be a family member who has been an outcast for years. Perhaps a lonely neighbor, or someone at work who just does not fit in.

The scope of the problems seems overwhelming. What can I as one person do for all of these? But that is just the point! If I as one person reach out to just one other person, and you as one person reach out to another, and another . . .

Sr. Ancilla Keinberger, O.P.

Jesus, may I always to ready to reach out to all the little ones in my life.

Give Generously

■ **One who sows sparingly will reap sparingly, and one who sows bountifully will reap bountifully.**
2 Corinthians 9:6

The ultimate gauge of our Christian commitment is our generosity. If we want to assess the genuineness of our discipleship, we need only look at our level of giving, for all other virtues are related to it. If my faith or love is weak, I will have problems opening my hand to share my resources with others. I will be afraid to give (time, resources, attention) because there might not be enough left for me. When I am more concerned about my welfare than about others, I am not trusting God's providence nor the charity of others—I am unable to believe that God will care for me.

On the other hand, the more I trust God, the more I am able to share generously, even to the point of giving my very life away, hour by hour, for others. There will be no flowers next summer if this year's plants do not give their blossoms.

Sr. Ruth Marlene Fox, O.S.B.

God loves a cheerful giver.
2 Corinthians 9:7

Merciful Love

■ **Should you not have dealt mercifully with your fellow servant, as I dealt with you?** Matthew 18:33

In every sphere of interpersonal relationships, justice must be corrected by love which is patient and kind, which possesses the characteristics of that merciful love that forms the essence of the Gospel and Christianity.

Merciful love is the basis of the Lord's answer to Peter's question about how many times to forgive others. In the symbolic language of the Bible, seventy times seven times means that we must be able to forgive everyone every time. Surely this is one of the most difficult and radical commands of the Gospel. Yet how much suffering and anguish, how much futility, destruction and violence would be avoided, if only we put into practice in all our human relationships the Lord's answer to Peter.

Pope John Paul II
Homily, New Orleans, 9/12/'87

There are three rules for dealing with other people: Kindness, kindness, kindness.

Fulton J. Sheen

Change Of Heart

■ **You shall love the Lord, your God, with all your heart, and with all your soul, and with all your strength.** Deuteronomy 6:5

It should be easy for us to love God, but for many of us it usually isn't. Many struggle to love God, but they are burdened by experiences that have hurt them. Through these experiences many people suffer from a lack of self-confidence, from fear, anger, hatred, envy and much more.

We store all of this psychic junk in our hearts, leaving little room for God. Yet God is there, although buried in our clutter. **We must earnestly ask God to help us clean house.** Getting rid of the trash can be a painful experience. But there can also be moments of joy in working with God to make space in our hearts for love. And the end result will be more wondrous than we could ever imagine.

Charlotte Rancilio

O God, help me to love you as I ought.

Prayer When Angry

■ **Why ever did I come out of the womb to see toil and sorrow and end my days in shame?** Jeremiah 20:18

If in my prayer I give voice to what is in my heart, then my prayer is genuine. If I separate my feelings into "nice" and "not nice" and then use only "nice" feelings in prayer, I attempt to pray a lie. The reason that Jeremiah's long prayer of woe strikes us as authentic is that he did not censor his feelings or his prayer.

Especially in grief people are tempted to censor their feelings and their prayer. How can I pray if I tell myself "I shouldn't feel this way"? The fact is, I *do* feel this way, and denying that fact undermines all my prayers. Sometimes the grieving person is ready to pray in anger, but someone else—like one of Job's friends—suggests, "You shouldn't feel that way." Fine, now the grieving person has to contend with grief plus the guilt for feeling that way . . . It's bad enough if I censor my own prayers, but trying to censor someone else's is even worse. Dispirited belief, agnosticism or atheism may result. What kind of God is so fragile as to need protection from honest expressions of human emotions? Is any God so fragile worth believing in?

Fr. Pat McCloskey, O.F.M.
When You Are Angry With God

Keeping Sight Of God

■ **When the disciples saw Jesus walking on the water, they were terrified. "It is a ghost!" they said, and in their fear they began to cry out.** Matthew 14:26

Even the disciples, who were weathered fishermen and sailors, were taken aback by the sudden storm in this gospel account. And then, at the sight of Jesus on the water, they panicked. They could not recognize the very Jesus they had been traveling with day and night. **In a moment of human terror they lost their awareness of God in their lives.**

When a person is not centered in God through daily prayer, faith becomes weakened, the ability to recognize God in the daily situations of life can be lost. It is through the steady faithfulness to prayer that our relationship with Christ becomes strong. It is through prayer that faith grows and flourishes. Through Him the waters are stilled. Through prayer we can see the Lord clearly, even on dark and stormy nights.

Lucia Godwin

Mary's Glory And Ours

■ **My being proclaims the greatness of the Lord, my spirit finds joy in God my savior, for he has looked upon his servant in her lowliness; all ages to come shall call me blessed.** Luke 1:46-48

Mary, in heaven and glorified, is for us a constant sign and cause of hope. We do not want to lose sight of her or forget that she is the same woman who lived a very ordinary human life in a little town called Nazareth, who didn't understand everything, even though her Son was God, living right with her, praying and reading the Scriptures with her. She had her questions and her fears. Our daily stumbling and bumbling does not separate us from our ultimate fulfillment and glorification.

Do you feel uncomfortable, as I do, in thinking about and speaking about your own glorification? We have been so schooled in adopting a hangdog humility before God that it is difficult for us to break free and really sing our own *Magnificat*. **We are destined to be glorious! The alternative is unthinkable.**

So we want to see Mary as a fellow traveler, one who can inspire, enlighten and encourage us on the way. Yet we want to see Mary in all her glory, in order to . . . let her be for us a source of hope.

Fr. M. Basil Pennington, O.C.S.O.
Mary Today

Jesus, Remember Me

■ **Jesus, remember me when you come into your kingdom.** Luke 23:42

This was the prayer of the penitent thief on the cross—and it must be our prayer too. Who can do us any good except the Lord, who shall also be our judge? When depressing thoughts about ourselves come into our minds and afflict us, "Jesus, remember me" is all that we have to say. We have "no work, nor reason, nor wisdom, nor knowledge" of our own to better ourselves. We can say nothing to God in defense of ourselves. We can but acknowledge that we are grievous sinnners, and addressing Him as suppliants, merely beg Him to bear us in mind in mercy. We can beg Him for Jesus' sake to do us some favor, not according to our merits, but for the love of Christ.

To whom should we go? Who can do us any good, except the One who was born into this world as our Savior, was bruised for our iniquities, and rose again for our salvation?

John Henry Newman
Kindly Light: A Cardinal Newman Prayerbook

Filled To The Brim

■ **My cup overflows.** Psalm 23:5

The Lord showers us daily with gifts, but if we are like an overturned cup, the gifts just fall to the side. If we would turn the glass over, if we would open our hearts and accept the gifts of God's love, peace, wisdom and fruitfulness, the glass could become filled.

Once we accept God's gifts and have experienced and cherished them, then only can we extend them to others—and it will not be difficult. Like an overflowing cup, there will be something that will just come forth from us. There will be love and peace that others will see just because we have accepted the Lord's gifts.

We need to take the first step, by opening our hearts to the Lord each day. Then we must act with confidence knowing that the Lord has answered our prayers by continuing to send us his gifts—all that we will ever really need to be his faithful servant. We will have been filled with all of God's love and peace, so much so that we will have no choice in offering the blessings we have to others.

Joyce S. Miller

Stone-Heartedness

■ **I will give you a new heart and place a new spirit within you, taking from your bodies your stony hearts and giving you natural hearts.** Ezekiel 36:26

Most people battle their way through life not asking the Lord what the divine will is, but determined to achieve their own goals and objectives. They don't really know how to turn it all over to God, how to surrender everything. They push and pressure to get what they want and they learn the hard way that life does not easily bend to their will.

Even so, they cling to their battle plan, convinced they are on the right path, following the right way. They do not really ask God to show them the divine desires. They may think they do but, in fact, they only turn to God to get support for carrying out their own plans. They want God to fit right in with their ideas, to make their dreams come true.

Fr. John Catoir
Enjoy the Lord

What does it profit you to give God one thing if God asks you for another? Consider what it is God wants, and then do it.

St. John of the Cross

The Rest Of Heaven

■ I heard a voice from heaven say, "Write this: Blessed are the dead who die in the Lord from now on." "Yes," said the Spirit, "let them find rest from their labors, for their works accompany them."

Revelation 14:13

Christ is already in that place of peace, which is all in all. He is on the right hand of God. He is hidden in the brightness of the radiance which issues from the everlasting Throne. He is in the very abyss of peace, where there is no voice of tumult or distress, but a deep stillness . . . the most perfect of joys, the utter, profound, ineffable tranquility of the Divine Essence. Christ has entered into his rest. O, how great a good it will be, if, when this troublesome life is over, we in our turn also enter into that same rest . . .

Here we are tossing upon the sea, and the wind is contrary. All through the day we are tried and tempted in various ways. We cannot think, speak or act except infirmity and sin are at hand. But in the unseen world where Christ has entered, all is peace . . .

That is our home. Here we are but on pilgrimage, and Christ is calling us home.

John Henry Newman
Kindly Light: A Cardinal Newman Prayerbook

Possessions

■ **If you seek perfection, go, sell your possessions and give to the poor. You will then have treasure in heaven. After that, come back and follow me.** Matthew 19:21

The guru sat in meditation on the riverbank when a disciple bent down to place two enormous pearls at his feet, a token of reverence and devotion.

The guru opened his eyes, lifted one of the pearls, and held it so carelessly that it slipped out of his hand and rolled down the bank into the river.

The horrified disciple plunged in after it,but, though he dove in again and again till late evening, he had no luck. Finally, wet and exhausted, he roused the guru from his meditation: "You saw where it fell. Show me the spot so I can get it back for you."

The guru lifted the other pearl, threw it into the river and said, "Right there!"

Do not attempt to possess things, for things cannot really be possessed. Only make sure you are not possessed by them and you will be the sovereign of creation.

Fr. Anthony de Mello, S.J.
The Heart of the Enlightened

Contentment

■ **The young man went away sad, for his possessions were many.** Matthew 19:22

Contentment never comes with merely **having,** regardless of its proportion, because having is external of our being, and peace resides within. **Unless we are happy on the inside, nothing on the outside can reach the depths of the soul.** Most discontent is over material things, which proves that they are sought more ardently than spiritual goods.

This does not mean that contentment is incompatible with an earnest desire to enlarge our provision of earthly things, in order to give blessings to those around us; nor does contentment mean sloth in business or neglect of worldy interests. Contentment is not the opposite of thrift and industry, but of covetousness and unbelieving anxiety.

Contentment is the gracious disposition of the mind, arising from absolute trust in God, so that the scales of our heart are equally poised in both prosperity and adversity.

Bishop Fulton J. Sheen
On Being Human

Mary, Queen Of Peace

■ **"Rejoice, O highly favored daughter! The Lord is with you. Blessed are you among women."** Luke 1:28

Virgin of the Rosary, our mother! Pray for us now. Grant to us the priceless gift of peace, of forgiving all wrongs and harboring no grudges, for the reconciliation of all people as brothers and sisters.

May violence and warfare cease. May dialogue grow and may people live in peace with each other. May new ways of justice and prosperity open up. We ask this of you whom we invoke as Queen of Peace now and at the hour of our death!

We entrust to you all the victims of injustice and violence, all those who have died in natural disasters, all those who at the hour of their death turn to you as mother and patron, so that with you we may glorify together the Father, the Son and the Holy Spirit. Amen.

Pope John Paul II
Draw Near to God

Tender Love

■ **May God our Father who loves us and in mercy gave us eternal consolation and hope, console your hearts and strengthen them for every good work and word.** 2 Thessalonians 2:16-17

Jesus came into this world for one purpose. He came to give us the good news that God loves us, that God is love, that God loves you and that God loves me. Jesus wants us to love one another as he loves each one of us. Let us love him. How did Jesus love you and me? By giving his life. He gave all that he had, his life, for you and me. He died on the cross because he loves us, and he wants us to love one another as he loves each one of us. When we look at the cross, we know how he loves us. When we look at the manger we know how he loves us, you and me, your family, my family and everybody's family with a tender love. And God loves us with a tender love. That is all that Jesus came to teach us, the tender love of God.

Mother Teresa
Jesus: The Word to be Spoken

Seeing & Being Seen

■ **"How do you know me?" Nathanael (Bartholomew) asked him. "Before Philip called you," Jesus answered, "I saw you under the fig tree."**

John 1:48

Do I want to be seen by Jesus? Do I want to be known by him? If I am ready with all my inner ambiguities, then a faith can grow which proclaims Jesus as the Son of God. Only such a faith can open my eyes. **I will see when I am willing to be seen.** I will receive new eyes that can see the mysteries of God's own life when I allow God to see me, all of me, even those parts that I do not want to see myself.

As I look into your eyes, O Lord Jesus, they frighten me because they pierce my innermost being like flames of fire. But they console me as well because flames are purifying and healing. Your eyes are so severe yet so loving, so unmasking yet so protecting, so penetrating yet so caressing, so profound yet so intimate, so distant yet so inviting.

I want to be seen by you, to dwell under your caring gaze, and to grow strong and gentle in your sight.

Fr. Henri J.M. Nouwen
The Road to Daybreak

Learning To Wait

■ **It is good that one should wait quietly for the salvation of the Lord.** Lamentations 3:26

There is nothing so humbling as waiting—that is why time was created, so that we might learn to wait. Waiting makes you feel inferior to the person who is keeping you waiting. And this begins to dawn on you the longer you have to wait. That is why some people cannot stand it anymore and get up and walk out.

But God has the right to make us wait not only for an hour, or a day, or a week, or a month, but our whole lifetime. By waiting we come to accept the fact that God is the Lord; we are only a creature, and whatever we have is His pure gift. Although He wants immensely to give us supernatural gifts, He is not going to make the same mistake—if that is the word for it—that He made with Adam. He will not give them until we have fully learned, tasted and accepted our lowliness and poverty.

Humility is the whole-hearted acceptance of the fact that God owes us nothing and that we owe Him everything. We must first learn to wait with patience.

Fr. Thomas Keating, O.C.S.O.
Crisis of Faith

Pride And Glory

■ **Pride goes before destruction, and a haughty spirit before a fall.** Proverbs 16:18

There was once a scientist who discovered the art of reproducing himself so perfectly that it was impossible to tell the reproduction from the original. One day he learned that the Angel of Death was searching for him, so he produced a dozen copies of himself. The angel was at a loss to know which of the thirteen specimens before him was the scientist, so he left them all alone and returned to heaven.

But not for long, for being an expert in human nature, the Angel came up with a clever device. He said, "Sir, you must be a genius to have succeeded in making such perfect reproductions of yourself. However, I have discovered a flaw in your work, just one tiny flaw."

Immediately, the scientist jumped out from among all the others and shouted, "Impossible. Where is the flaw?"

"Right here," said the Angel, picking up the scientist from the reproductions and carrying him off.

Fr. Anthony de Mello, S.J.
Taking Flight

Expect Trials

■ **Endure your trials as the discipline of God, who deals with you as sons. For what son is there whom his father does not discipline?** Hebrews 12:7

Christians expect suffering because Jesus has specifically told us to. He was the man of sorrows, and his best people throughout the ages have always suffered the most. **"The cross is the gift God gives to friends,"** said St. Philip Neri.

The point of our lives in this world is not comfort, security, or even happiness, but training; not fulfillment but preparation. It's a lousy home, but it's a fine gymnasium. It is an uphill bowling alley. The point is not to reach the pins, the goal. "One step forward, one backward" is our law here. Progress is a myth. The stronger we get, the weaker we get, the more dependent on our crutches, our machines. For we misunderstand where we are if we believe in earthly utopias. The universe is a soul-making machine, a womb, an egg. Jesus didn't make it into a rose garden when he came, though he could have. Rather, he wore the thorns from his world's gardens.

If we believe that, **we will expect sufferings rather than resent them as a scandal.**

Peter Kreeft
Making Sense Out of Suffering

The Making Of Saints

■ **We always mention you in our prayers and thank God for you all, and constantly remember before God our Father how you have shown your faith in action, worked for love and persevered through hope, in our Lord Jesus Christ.** 1 Thessalonians 1:2-3

St. Augustine once asked God to make him chaste—but "not yet." This reminder of Augustine's fraility helps us remember that those we now revere as saints were once somebody's neighbor or boss or mother-in-law, that they were not universally liked, nor untouched by uncertainty and failure. We might prefer to think otherwise, but their virtue was won much as ours is: in the day-to-day choice to live as Jesus did.

St. Augustine's circuitous path to the heart of Jesus gives comfort to those of us who can't imagine that our daily efforts are steps along that same journey. Augustine reminds us that, no matter the false starts, the search for faith, the willingness to love and perseverance in hope will ultimately lead us home.

Sharon T. Santia

Use the world, do not let the world use you. You have entered the world on a journey. You came here only to depart from here, not to remain. St. Augustine

Recesses Of The Heart

■ **This people pays me lip service, but their heart is far from me.** Mark 7:6

Jesus warns us that outward conformity to human precepts is no guarantee of holiness; it is the hidden recesses of the heart which reveal what we are. There, in those places known to God alone, lie attitudes and desires which may very well contradict our outward behavior. We need to place less emphasis on outer observances and to pay more attention to forming hearts which are truly pleasing to God.

By conforming to what church, state and local customs require of us, we can easily feel self-satisfied. In the world's eyes—and in our own—we are good Christians, citizens and neighbors. We can measure our worth by our observance of rules, regulations and traditions, and by all the extras we do besides. "Doing," of course, has its place or nothing would ever get done and anarchy would reign. But we need to remember that it is our hearts for which our God hungers and nothing less.

Elizabeth-Anne Vanek

Count Your Blessings

■ **Give thanks in all circumstances, for this is the will of God in Christ Jesus for you.** 1 Thessalonians 5:18

Father, we are sometimes reminded to count our blessings, to recognize the gifts You have given us through Jesus Christ. It would be impossible to actually count them, for everything we have and are is a gift from You. There is nothing in our lives that has not been given. We ask Your grace to have the strength to offer all these gifts back to You, to use them for Your honor and glory, for the good of others rather than for ourselves. Too often we have squandered Your gifts on our own pleasure, for our own selfishness, without thought that we are wasting what You had given us. Renew in us the determination to give all that we are, day by day, for love of You. Help us to hold back nothing, to waste nothing of the good things You have given us.

Fr. Killian Speckner
The Prayers of Father Killian

Giving And Receiving

■ **We are God's co-workers; you are God's cultivation, his building.** 1 Corinthians 3:9

We don't like to envision ourselves as greedy, grasping takers. We prefer to see ourselves as cheerful givers—co-workers with God in the world today. After all, Jesus gave us his all—his word, his healing touch, and his very life. Also we read of the apostles and saints who gave willingly of themselves to minister to us, God's people.

But perhaps we find ourselves giving not because it is better but easier than receiving. How can this be? Receiving brings indebtedness—a need to respond with a "thank you" to another. And those "thank yous" can be so difficult!

It's easy to forget that the apostles and saints could do God's work only after having opened themselves to God's gift of love. They recognized the importance of a gracious acceptance—a "thank you." We, too, can't give that which we haven't first acknowledged we've received. God has given us divine love, both directly and through the words and touch of those around us. Gracious acceptance enhances our ability to give.

Mary H. Rea

Seeking God

■ **Such are the people who seek God, who seek the face of the God of Jacob.** Psalm 24:6

We seek the face of God. We want to experience God, feel close to God, know the warm security of God's presence. God becomes settled, nestled in our hearts and minds. At times this is good and as it should be.

But there are other times when we must be aware of God unsettling us, of God moving us from complacency to further action. God's presence can be keenly felt in times of chaos and turmoil, precisely when we think that God is absent. It is at those times that the sharing in Jesus' passion and death occurs. We would rather experience the resurrection; but we must first seek God in the very turmoil that engulfs us.

The God that we seek is no one-sided person, no fair-weather friend. The God we seek experiences all of our lives with us and uses these experiences to bring us closer to the divine heart.

Jean Royer

Tears are to wisdom what rain is to flowers.

Self-Knowledge

■ **No servant can serve two masters. Either he will hate the one and love the other or be attentive to the one and despise the other. You cannot give yourself to God and money.** Luke 16:13

Sharpen your wants and express them . . .

How good it is to know what I want, that is, to allow myself to realize what it is that I really want, to feel it keenly, then to manifest it simply to the person from whom I want it, leaving the other at the same time entirely free to grant my wish or refuse it. **This is an exercise in self-knowledge, freedom, humility, courage and sincerity.** The wonder is that most of the time when we ask a concrete thing from a concrete person, we get it. And if we don't get it, we have lost nothing. And in any case we grow in clarity and strength.

We may also apply that principle to spiritual discernment, as expressed in this saying: "To find out what God wants of you, first find out what you want of God."

Fr. Carlos G. Valles, S.J.
Mastering Sadhana

To find out what God wants of you,
first find out what you want of God.

Lost Shepherd

■ **Conduct your affairs with humility, and you will be loved more than a giver of gifts. Humble yourself the more, the greater you are, and you will find favor with God.** Sirach 3:17-18

Bishop Fulton J. Sheen often told audiences about an incident in Philadelphia when he was visiting there for a speech at Town Hall. He had left his hotel early enough to walk a bit. After strolling for a while, he realized he had lost his way. He noticed a group of boys playing in the street and approached them.

"I'm a stranger in your city and I seem to have lost my way. Can you please tell me the way to Town Hall?"

One of the boys volunteered, and instructed him on how to get there. Then the boy asked, "What are you going to do there?"

Sheen replied, "I'm going to deliver a lecture."

"On what?" asked the boy.

"On how to get to heaven," said Sheen.

"To heaven?" exclaimed the youngster. "You don't even know how to get to Town Hall!"

Bishop Fulton J. Sheen
The Wit & Wisdom of Bishop Fulton Sheen

A Time To Awake

■ **We do not want you to be unaware about those who have fallen asleep, so that you may not grieve like the rest, who have no hope.** 1 Thessalonians 4:13

I must die to be born. The body must die because it has served its purpose and is worn out, like the placenta . . . It is good that the body gets worn out. It is even good that it ages before it dies, for that makes it easier for us to abandon it . . . we learn from detachment from the old womb when the time for birth approaches.

Reincarnation would be intolerable, like repeating kindergarten, or having triplets at age 50, or hearing the same symphony twelve times in a row. Enough is enough. **We need not repeat the dream of life but to wake up.** "One short sleep past, we wake eternally" (John Donne).

Those who catch a glimpse of the next life, whether by mysticism, divine revelation or resuscitation, always use images of waking, not of sleep . . . The Book of Revelation says of heaven, "There is no night there."

Peter J. Kreeft
Love Is Stronger Than Death

Carpenter's Son

■ **The Son of Man is going to be handed over to men and they will kill him . . .** Matthew 17:22-23

Carpenter's son, carpenter's son,
is the wood fine
and smoothly sanded, or rough-grained,
lying along your back? Was it well-planed?
Did they use
a plumbline
when they set you up? Is the angle true?
Why did they choose
that dark, expensive stain
to gloss the timbers
next to your feet and fingers? You
should know—who,
Joseph-trained, judged all trees
for special service.
Carpenter's son, carpenter's son,
were the nails new and cleanly driven
when the dark hammers sang?
Is the earth warped from where you hang,
high enough for a
world view?
Carpenter's son, carpenter's son,
was it a job well done?

Luci Shaw
"Craftsman"
from *The Secret Trees*

Changing Customs

■ **Immediately she rose and waited on them.**
Luke 4:39

At the time of Jesus it was not customary for a woman to wait on men, unless they were members of the household. So a visiting rabbi would be greeted and served by the male head of house. His wife would not even appear. How different is this Gospel story!

Luke tells us that Jesus stood over Peter's ailing mother-in-law and rebuked the fever, and it left her. Mark, who was close to Peter, an eyewitness of the event, tells that Jesus took her by the hand and helped her up. To touch a woman other than one's wife was against the Jewish law. But Jesus knew no law where charity was concerned. And the one he healed? She joyfully responded in kind. Her heart reached out in gratitude and she herself served the guests.

The lesson is clear. **When we are healed of our infirmity, we are not to return to our everyday routines.** We are not to be bound by former restrictions that would limit the liberty of the children of God. We are to follow the example of Peter's mother-in-law and put our gift at the service of the Church.

Sr. Mary Catherine Vukmanic, O.S.U.

Shades Of Gray

■ A good man produces goodness from the good in his heart, an evil man produces evil out of his store of evil. Each man speaks from his heart's abundance.

Luke 6:45

We know that we come in shades of gray, that we are a mix of black and white, good and bad—even though some people may appear to be the heroes and heroines while others seem to be the villians. We are all capable of doing good or evil. When we sin, we do not necessarily draw inspiration from the depths of hell but from the evil in our own hearts. Jesus tells us that we act mostly from our heart's abundance.

If our hearts are filled with mostly good, most of our actions will bring forth goodness. We should not dwell on our sins but seek forgiveness and use the sinful experience as an aid in trying to rid our hearts of the evil that dwells there.

As St. Paul did, we must remember that we are indeed sinners, but **forgiven** sinners. "Christ came into the world to save sinners. Of these, I myself am the worst. But on that very account I was dealt with more mercifully." (1 Tm. 1:15)

Charlotte Rancilio

Lord, have mercy on me, a sinner.

Waiting For God

■ **We know that God makes all things work together for the good of those who have been called according to his decree.** Romans 8:28

In her response to God at the time of Annunciation, Mary was saying, "I don't know what this all means, but I trust that good things will happen." She trusted so deeply that her waiting was open to all possibilities. She did not want to control them. She believed that when she listened carefully, she could trust what was to happen.

Waiting open-endedly is an enormously radical attitude toward life. And so is trusting something that will happen to us that is far beyond our own imaginings. So, too, is giving up control over our future and letting God define our life, trusting that God molds us according to God's love and not according to our fear. The spiritual life is a life in which we wait, actively present to the moment, trusting that new things will happen to us, new things that are far beyond our own imagination, fantasy or prediction. That indeed, is a very radical stance toward life in a world preoccupied with control.

Fr. Henri J. M. Nouwen
Seeds of Hope

Mary, blessed Mother, help me to be open and receptive to what God wants in my life.

God's Love For Me

■ **You shall love your neighbor as yourself.**

Romans 13:9

How do we love ourselves? To many of us, the concept of self-love may seem foreign, uncomfortable. Perhaps we were trained to overextend ourselves, to say "yes" unconditionally to those in need of our time, talents and resources or to sacrifice our own interests to the common good. Perhaps we learned false humility with the result that we can barely see our own gifts, let alone our goodness. Perhaps we were so deprived of love that we have grown up seeing others as more worthwhile, more lovable. How could they—or God—see anything of value in us?

Unless we love ourselves fully, we cannot know God's love or what it means to love another human being. Love of self is the starting point. It means accepting the gift of one's life with open hands, knowing that God loves us in weakness and folly as well as strength and beauty. When we experience God's love for us, then we, in turn, are filled with a love so strong that it radiates toward those around us. This kind of love, writes Paul, is the fulfillment of the law.

Elizabeth-Anne Vanek

Help me, dear God, to know and appreciate your love for me.

Staying In Touch

■ **Jesus went out to the mountain to pray, spending the night in communion with God.** Luke 6:12

Decisions! Decisions! Sometimes I get so tired of making decisions, Lord! As soon as I make up my mind on one issue, another rears its head. I can't even opt out, for to choose not to decide is a decision. How am I supposed to know what is best? Even when I have sufficient time to garner facts, weigh alternatives, ask advice, I'm still unsure my decision was right.

The decisions that confronted you were far weightier than any I will ever face. How did you always know what to do? When it came time to establish your Church, how did you know which men to choose? How many? What to say to them? St. Luke says that you prepared by spending the whole night in communion with God. Attuned to God at all times, you followed the Father's promptings. In your busiest moments, you had only to turn inward to find your Father there.

So, Lord, I have but one decision to make, namely, to remain close enough to you that I know your will.

Sr. Mary Charleen Hug, S.N.D.

Graceful Moments

■ Indeed, the whole crowd was trying to touch him because power went out from him which cured all.

Luke 6:19

Jesus assures his disciples in every age that if they are sincere in their efforts to follow him, they will do greater works than he did. It follows, then, that healing power goes out of me, as well—and more frequently than I notice its going.

Whenever I do take a moment to think how I've met Jesus in my day, I often recall a chance encounter with someone that had a surprising element in it. Perhaps the person inadvertently gave me a piece of information I needed. Perhaps something I said, which I regarded rather commonplace, proved to be very encouraging or enlightening to them.

Now and then I discover an extra something on my shelf that has escaped my sporadic "weedings out" and suddenly is available for the very person at my door that day. Healing energy hums in these graced encounters. My challenge is to notice the energy flow as these moments happen so that I become more adept at recognizing the power of God moving out of and into me each day.

Sr. Audrey Synnott, R.S.M.

Waiting For The Lord

■ **I have waited, waited for the Lord.** Psalm 40:2

We are not a people who like to wait. We want short lines, immediate results, punctual transportation, instant replays. We are do-ers and fixers, more at home with active involvement than passive waiting. Many times the proper response is to move, solve, take charge, act. Yet, at other times, the Lord seems to be saying to us, "Wait. Wait without squirming; wait when you don't feel like it; wait in the darkness; wait even if you don't know what you are waiting for."

And so we wait for the showing forth of the Lord, whether in our interior or exterior lives. Since God is neither capricious nor malicious, the waiting is not a punishment but a grace. It is an opportunity to stand before the mystery of God's timing and movement in our lives—totally incomprehensible and yet overwhelmingly exquisite for those who have waited until the appointed hour.

Nancy F. Summers

Jesus, I hate to wait. I almost get in a panic when I have to sit and bide my time rather than move ahead. Help me learn patience, help me to wait for you.

Looking Ahead

■ **Vanity of vanities, says Qoheleth, vanity of vanities! All things are vanity!** Ecclesiastes 1:2

The earth no longer interests me. I am weary of it. It gives me increasingly less pleasure. I remain just as long as I need to remain in order to learn to love, to pay something toward the cost of the redemption, but it no longer attracts me as it once did. I have come to realize that it is in my interest to move on. And this is an important sign.

I am familiar with the changing seasons of life, I have lived through its loves, I have rejoiced in each as it dawned. Now I am looking round for yet other seasons, for another love, for another dawn.

I have lived down here long enough to convince myself that we were not made for the earth, that the earth is not our paradise, and that it has been of service to us only as a great preparation for something else. Above all, it carries within it the all-too-familiar seeds of decay, and as the years pass I find it increasingly wearisome, while my soul fixes its sights with assurance on the One who always has the power to captivate, the uniquely, truly and eternally new: God.

Carlo Carretto
In Search of the Beyond

Saying 'Yes' To Life

■ **He humbled himself, obediently accepting even death, death on a cross! Because of this God highly exalted him and bestowed on him the name above every other name.** Philippians 2:8-9

Every time we open a newspaper with all its stories of war, murder, kidnapping, torture, battering and countless other tragedies that lead to sickness and death, we are faced with the temptation to believe that, after all, death is victorious. But time and time again the death of Jesus, the Holy One, calls us to choose for life. **The great challenge of the Christian life is to say "Yes" to life even in the smallest and, seemingly, unimportant details.** Every moment there is a choice to be made: the choice for or against life. Do I choose to think about a person in a forgiving or in an accusing way? Do I choose to speak a word of acceptance or a word of rejection? Do I choose to reach out or to hold back, to share or to hoard, to yield or to cling, to hurt or to heal? Even the deeper emotions of our heart are subject to such choices. I can choose to be resentful or grateful, despairing or hopeful, sad or glad, angry or peaceful.

Fr. Henri J. M. Nouwen
Walk With Jesus: Stations of the Cross

Compassionate Concern

■ **He said to the disciple, "There is your mother." From that hour onward, the disciple took her into his care.** John 19:27

Jesus reached out to comfort his sorrowing mother and his beloved disciple even during his final agony on the cross. The Gospel doesn't record a response from either John or Mary. Perhaps neither spoke. But if I close my eyes and put myself into the scene, I can imagine each of them reaching out to console the other. John may have placed his arm around Mary and drawn her close. Perhaps she whispered a few words of loving concern to him.

Often we feel that we have no words to comfort those who have lost loved ones. We simply don't know what to say. Flowery words and gushing emotion aren't necessary. A simple, "I love you," or "I'm here for you," will let them know we care. When we find ourselves unable to utter even those few words, a touch or a hug can also convey our loving concern. When we reach out and share the sorrow of others, we reflect Christ's compassion and caring for us all.

Mary H. Rea

A Forgiving Heart

■ **Forgive your neighbor's injustice; then when you pray, your own sins will be forgiven.** Sirach 28:2

When I pray the Lord's prayer, I often call to mind the faces of those who have hurt me the most, especially those with whom reconciliation is impossible. I pause briefly and study the images which surface; then, when I am conscious of having a place for each person in my heart, I move on. "And lead us not into temptation . . ."

It is difficult praying for those who have wronged us when, like Lear, we consider ourselves more sinned against than sinning or when we still suffer from the effects of the wrongs inflicted upon us. **But the forgiving heart is a liberated heart.** When we reach out and embrace another in spite of our pain, the more deeply we understand the lavishness of God's love. We let go the desire for any righting of wrongs or making amends and simply accept the offender unconditionally. In this forgiving embrace we are most like God.

Elizabeth-Anne Vanek

Cycles Of Compassion

■ **He deserves to have you do this for him, for he loves our nation and he built the synagogue for us.**

Luke 7:4-5

One act of compassion for the welfare of another person grows into a cycle of concern. The Roman centurion in this Gospel story is concerned about his dying servant and so sends some Jewish elders to petition Jesus for healing. In turn, the Jewish elders have particular concern for the centurion because of his past generosity toward them.

Jesus responds immediately by setting out for the centurion's home. For his part, the centurion shows his concern by not wanting to inconvenience Jesus any more than is necessary. Completing the cycle of compassion initiated by the centurion, Jesus heals the servant.

One act of kindness or concern shown to another person most often generates a second and a third with ripples continuing on into infinity. We will never know how one act of concern for another—though it may seem insignificant to us—multiplies in a continuous cycle of compassion.

Sr. Ruth Marlene Fox, O.S.B.

Life Within

■ **To you, Yahweh, I call; my Rock, hear me. If you do not listen, I shall become like those who are dead.**

Psalm 28:1

If you watch your life carefully, you will discover quite soon that we hardly ever live from within outward. Instead we respond to incitement, to excitement. In other words, we live indirectly, by reaction. Something happens and we respond, someone speaks and we answer.

But when we are left without anything that stimulates us to think, speak or act, we realize that there is very little in us that will prompt us to action in any direction at all.

This is really a very dramatic discovery. We are completely empty, we do not act from within ourselves, but accept as our life a life which is actually fed in from outside. We are used to things happening which compel us to do other things. How seldom can we live simply by means of the depth and the richness that we try to assure ourselves we have.

Metropolitan Anthony
Daily Readings

Heal Me, Dear Lord!

■ **Then will the eyes of the blind be opened, the ears of the deaf be cleared.** Isaiah 35:5

I have hearing, Lord, but I am deaf. I have sight, but I am blind. You came to heal all those with disabilities and I am one of them. Yes, I have the gift of physical wholeness, but I do not always see and hear and understand. I ask you now to unseal my ears and to open my eyes. I ask you to let me grow in awareness that I may see what is below the surface, that I may hear what is barely audible, that I may perceive what is almost imperceptible. Give me the gift of being awake, Lord. Jolt me out of apathy and indifference. Startle me out of my comfortable routine. Rouse me from all that buries me under blankets of habit.

Yes, Lord, I know there will be a price to pay. Yes, I know that reality can burn and that it is more comfortable not to see and not to hear. But I also know that sharper seeing and keener hearing will lead me to your life. Heal me, Lord. Comfort my frightened heart.

Elizabeth-Anne Vanek

Prayer In Darkness

■ **I lie prostrate in the dust; give me life according to your word.** Psalm 119:25

Lord, the silence in my soul is deafening. Prayers dash themselves against an impregnable wall. You dwell just beyond that wall. Joy spends itself, dissolving into fear and doubt. Peace chases worry and conflict. Love vanishes, for I am distant from its author. How spiritually dry I am!

I am waiting, Lord. Waiting for your joy to uplift me. For your light to be rekindled in my dark soul. For your pervading peace. For your steadfast love. Waiting for you to possess me again.

Come, Dearest Lord, enfold me in your arms and abolish the pain of my separation from you.

Virginia Ulrich

O Lord, grant me the serenity to accept what I cannot change, the courage to change what needs to be changed, and the wisdom to know the difference.

Loving Faith

■ **What good is it to profess faith without practicing it? Such faith has no power to save one, has it?**

James 2:14

What is meant by loving all is to feel well-disposed to all, to be ready to assist them, and to act toward those who come in our way as if we loved them. We cannot love those about whom we know nothing—except as we view them in Christ, as the objects of his atonement, that is, rather in faith than in love. Besides, love is a habit, and cannot be obtained without actual *practice*, which on so large a scale is impossible. We see then how absurd it is when writers talk magnificently about loving the whole human race with a comprehensive affection, of being the friends of all mankind. Such vaunting professions, what do they come to? That such people have certain benevolent feelings toward the world—feelings and nothing more—nothing more than unstable feelings . . . sure to fail in the hour of need. This is not to love others, it is but to talk about love. The real love of others *must* depend on practice, and so must begin by exercising itself on our friends around us.

John Henry Newman
Prayers, Poems, Meditations

The Child Within

■ **Whoever welcomes a child such as this for my sake welcomes me.** Mark 9:37

A trend popular in both spirituality and psychology is to recover the "inner child" so that one can function as a fully integrated adult. The inner child is that part of the self which is most truly who we are, the self we were created to be. Somewhere between childhood and the coming of age, we lose our childhood innocence and begin to play adult games: we wear masks to disguise our vulnerability; we push ourselves to forge ahead; we control events to get our way, we forget how to play and choose "career paths" instead of following our hearts. By allowing that inner child to resurface, by healing that child's wounds and reverencing that child's wisdom, we relearn the way of simplicity.

Jesus uses the child as an image of holiness, presenting a child to his disciples during their squabble over status. He identifies himself with the child, gently showing the hollowness of his friends' values and ambitions. Let us, too, learn from this child. Let us, too, open our arms to embrace the reality the child represents.

Elizabeth-Anne Vanek

Looking Inward

■ **Hypocrite, remove the plank from your own eye first; then you will see clearly enough to remove the speck from your brother's eye.** Luke 6:42

Did you ever get a speck of dust in your eye? The eye tears and one's vision is blurred. The tiny speck becomes a major annoyance and we must stop everything to get rid of it. I think Jesus is suggesting that we need to treat our inner "I" the same way.

Often, what we find most annoying in another person is identical to some feature within ourselves. Psychology calls it "projection"—the attribution of one's own feelings, ideas or attitudes to other people. Jesus speaks of a "plank." Either way, vision is blurred and we fail to see inward. We think it is easier to "fix" or correct the other person, but the only one I can change is myself.

What is it that angers or irritates me about that other person in my life right now? What is it that I want to change about him or her? Jesus tells us to look inward, to see if perhaps that habit or personality trait is lodged within us. Perhaps Jesus is saying, "Remove that tendency from your own 'I' first; then you will see clearly enough to help someone else."

Sr. Anita Constance, S.C.

The True Religion

■ **Who shall dwell on your holy mountain? Those whose way of life is blameless, who always do what is right, who speak the truth from their heart.**

Psalm 15:1-3

When asked which was the true religion, the Teacher replied with this story: Once there was a magic ring which gave its bearer the gifts of grace, kindness and generosity. When the owner of the ring was on his deathbed, each of his three sons came separately and asked him for the ring. The old man promised the ring to each of them. The man then sent for the finest jeweler in the land, and paid him to make two identical rings. Before he died, the man gave each son a ring without telling the others.

Later they discovered each had a ring. So they went to a judge to help determine who had the magic ring. He could not tell the difference, but said, "Why must we decide now? We shall know who has the magic ring when we observe the direction your life takes."

Each of the brothers then acted as if he had the magic ring by being kind, honest and thoughtful.

Religions are like these brothers. The moment their members stop striving for justice and love we will know their religion isn't the one God gave.

William R. White
Stories for the Journey

Avoiding Bitterness

■ **"Naked I came forth from my mother's womb and naked I go back again. The Lord gave and the Lord has taken away; blessed be the name of the Lord."**

Job 1:21

Why can some people call out, "blessed be the name of the Lord," in the midst of their suffering while others can only nurse a heart of bitterness? Why is it that some discover the redemptive value of suffering while others find no meaning? Part of the answer to these questions is an energizing gift we call faith. **Faith teaches us the art of suffering.**

We are blessed if we can be like that child that Jesus offers us as a model. A child, like Jesus on the cross, is not too sophisticated to cry out in the midst of suffering, but the child has not yet learned how to contain bitterness. The child is too close to the womb, fresh and new, still damp with the breath of life. Another model for creative suffering comes to us from Etty Hillesum who in the midst of the prison of a concentration camp writes, "It still all comes down to the same thing: life is beautiful and I believe in God. I want to be there right in the middle of what people call 'horror' and still say: life is beautiful . . . I am not afraid to look suffering straight in the eye."

Sr. Macrina Wiederkehr, O.S.B.

Good News Of God's Love

■ **Jesus now called the Twelve together and gave them power and authority to overcome all demons and to cure diseases. He sent them forth to proclaim the reign of God and heal the afflicted.** Luke 9:1-2

Jesus placed so great an emphasis on healing because the people had the wrong idea about God. They believed disease, infertility, poverty and the like were heavenly punishment. God, they thought, sat in judgment of those on earth, meting out afflictions to sinners and their children. Only by following the Mosaic law carefully could they avoid divine wrath.

Jesus came to tell us the good news: God loves us. Period. God shows us the Way, then steps back and lets us choose our own path. Fortunately, God does not love us only when we do the proper deeds or observe the correct laws. Nor do we have to earn the Creator's love by bearing with diseases or other "acts of God."

By a free decision for all time, God loves us. As an act of gratitude—not payment—we may freely submit to divine sovereignty and try to live according to the gospel. That same gospel tells us no matter what path we take, we have a compassionate father awaiting our return.

Laurie Kozisek

Job's Prayer

■ **After this, Job opened his mouth and cursed his day.** Job 3:1

Job was a good man who lost his large family and who was afflicted with boils from head to toe. Don't we all blame God as Job did, at least a little bit, when things go wrong? We hope that if we are faithful we will be healthy and prosperous.

But suffering is a mystery to which we do not have the answer, a mystery which will be with us our whole life long, despite how faithful we become. Injustice, chance, accidents, and wrong choices all cause suffering.

So if today my sister is ill or I hear bad news from any source, I may begin, as Job did, by cursing the day. God will not begrudge us our spontaneous outburst, our spontaneous curses. After all, in the Book of Job God says Job spoke rightly about pain and about divine realities. But like Job, we must quickly move on past our curses into prayer—prayer for awareness of God's healing presence in the midst of our suffering.

Sr. Marguerite Zralek, O.P.

My God, spare me the pain —but if it must be, give me the courage to face it gracefully.

Keeping One's Balance

■ **You must hold fast to faith, be firmly grounded and steadfast in it, unshaken in the hope promised you by the gospel you have heard.** Colossians 1:23

Even though everything turns and changes around us, we must always remain unchanging and ever looking, striving, and aspiring toward God. No matter what course the ship may take, no matter whether it sails to the east, west, north, or south, no matter what wind drives it on, the mariner's needle never points in any direction except toward the fair polar star. . . .

This absolute resolution never to forsake God and never to abandon his merciful love serves our soul as a counterweight to keep it in a holy equilibrium amid all the inequality of the various changes brought to it by the conditions of this life. When caught out in the fields by a storm little bees pick up small stones so that they can keep their balance in the air and not be easily carried away by the wind. So also when our soul has made its resolution and firmly embraced God's precious love, it keeps steady amid the inconstancy and change that come from consolations and afflictions, whether spiritual or temporal and whether exterior or interior.

St. Francis de Sales
Introduction to the Devout Life

Unavoidable Suffering

■ **Jesus began to teach them that the Son of Man had to suffer much, be rejected by the elders, the chief priest, and the scribes, be put to death , and rise three days later.** Mark 8:31

Our affluent society does all it can to do away with the reality of suffering. In the eyes of those who are blind to the transcendent, suffering and pain are incompatible with happiness. Funeral homes make it their profession to blur suffering. Medical science alleviates pain, the drug commercials on television advertise their pain killers and sleeping pills, and dope peddlers make it possible to escape a harsh reality. Not all of this is bad. It is a service to alleviate pain, to arrange a worthy funeral, and to pray to God for help when we suffer.

However, we should regard as unChristian an attitude which desires at all cost or with dubious means (drug abuse) to do away with both mental and physical suffering that is unavoidable! Since our lives are patterned after the life, death and resurrection of our Lord, we should in faith be willing to die with him—die to our egotistic selves, which is a painful process, and accept unavoidable suffering—in order to live with him forever.

Fr. John C. Kersten, S.V.D.
Bible Meditations For Every Day

Praise For Divine Mercy

■ As a young rabbi was walking alone under the stars, he suddenly knelt and prayed, "O Lord, let me never stray from you." But a voice from heaven said, "If I granted your request, how could I ever show you my mercy."

Bless Yahweh, O my soul. Bless God's holy name, all that is in me! Bless Yahweh, O my soul, and remember God's faithfulness; in forgiving all your offenses, in healing all your diseases, in redeeming your life from destruction, in crowning you with love and compassion, in filling your years with good things, in renewing your youth like an eagle's. . .

Yahweh's wrath does not last forever; it exists a short time only. We are never threatened, never punished as our guilt and our sins deserve. As the heights of heaven over earth so is the greatness of Yahweh's faithful love for those who fear God. Yahweh takes our sins away farther than the east is from the west. As tenderly as parents treat their children, so Yahweh has compassion on those who fear God.

Psalm 103:1-5, 9-13

Dead Weight

■ **There was a rich man who dressed in purple garments and fine linen and dined sumptuously each day. And lying at his door was a poor man named Lazarus.** Luke 16:19-20

In Vienna the emperors of the Austro-Hungarian Empire were buried in a Capuchin friary. When the funeral procession arrived, the grand duke would ceremoniously knock at the locked doors of the friary. A little window would open and the head monk would say, "Who is it?" The duke would answer something like this, "Franz Joseph, emperor of the Holy Roman Empire, king of Hungary, margrave of such and such." The answer would come back, "We do not know him." So the grand duke would knock again. "Who is there?" "Franz Joseph, his most Catholic imperial majesty, elector of the Pope, and so on and so on." And the answer would come again, "We don't know him." The duke would knock a third time and was asked again who was there. Then the grand duke would say, "Franz Joseph, a wretched sinner who seeks a place to lay his bones."

Then the door would open. Only in death do some face the need to rid ourselves of the world's vanity. Why can't we get over our vanities sooner!

Fr. Benedict J. Groeschel, C.F.R.
Stumbling Blocks or Stepping Stones

Worrywarts

■ **Even the hairs of your head are counted! Fear nothing.** Luke 12:7

Worry is the great spoiler. So many times when we could be celebrating the good things in our life we are instead lost in our worries about the future.

The Bible repeatedly urges us to trust God, to live as if we really believe that God will take care of the future. But trusting God is not easy for most of us, no matter how much we give lip service to the idea. It means placing our future into the hands of another, losing control of our own lives. That is too much for many of us; we would rather indulge in that preventive magic called worry. Some of us even take a perverse pride in worrying and try to assure ourselves that it is a virtue.

Still, if this awareness just gives us another thing to worry about, what good is that? We must not worry about our worrying! Rather, in prayer we must daily let go of our worries, turn them over to God, and let God help us learn to enjoy life more fully.

Joan Zrilich

Who says worrying does no good? All the bad things I worry about never happen!

Keeping Commitments

■ **Will you not stop twisting the straight paths of the Lord?** Acts 13:10

There is a story about a man faced with such difficulty that he prayed on his knees for days on end that God would save him. In his prayer he vowed that if rescued from his distress, he would sell his home and give all the money from the sale to the poor. Now it came to pass that his prayer was heard and the grave problem was resolved. But now that the trouble had passed, the man had second thoughts about his vow. Since his home was worth a great deal of money, he devised a plan. He would place his home for sale but on the condition that the buyer must also purchase his cat. He had little difficulty selling his home and the cat that went with it. The home he sold for $100 and the cat for $199,900. The money from the house he gave to the poor, and the money from the sale of the cat he kept for himself!

Fr. Edward Hays
In Pursuit of the Great White Rabbit

O God, forgive me for the times I have tried to slip out of my commitments with legalistic tricks.

The Illusion Of Greatness

■ **They stripped off his clothes . . .** Matthew 27:28

The stripped body of Jesus reveals to us the immense degradation that human beings suffer all through the world, at all places and in all times. Often I think of life as a journey to the mountaintop where I will see at last the full beauty of my surroundings and where I will experience myself in full possession of all my senses. But Jesus points in the other direction. Life is an increasing call to let go of desires, of success and accomplishment, to give up the need to be in control, to die to the illusion of greatness. The joy and peace that Jesus offers is hidden in the descending way of the cross. There lie hope, victory, and new life, but they are given to us where we are losing all.

I should not be afraid to lose, nor afraid for those who have lost much, if not all. Jesus was stripped so that we would dare to embrace our own poverty and the poverty of our humanity. In looking at our improvished selves and at the poverty of our fellow human beings, we come to discover the immense compassion that God shows to us.

Fr. Henri J.M. Nouwen
Walk With Jesus: Stations of the Cross

A Prayer For Trust

■ **Do not let your hearts be troubled. You have faith in God; have faith also in me.** John 14:1

Jesus, you have told us many times, in many different ways, to trust in you, to have faith in you. If you had not given us that gift of faith, we would be wandering on the earth, looking for you without knowing what we were looking for. We would have been empty people, ghostly people. We treasure that gift despite all of our fickleness and all of our weakness. In this prayer, we hold that gift out to you: make it stronger, more trusting. When it is so dark that we can't see this gift with us, let us trust; let us believe. We have committed ourselves to you, we have dedicated our lives to you. And though we have failed in so many ways, so many times, we trust in your love and forgiveness; we trust that you will renew our faith and let us be yours in every way, now and forever.

Fr. Killian Speckner
The Prayers of Father Killian

'Masters Of The Universe'

■ **Then Job answered the Lord and said: . . . I have dealt with great things that I do not understand; things too wonderful for me, which I cannot know. I had heard of you by word of mouth, but now my eye has seen you. Therefore, I disown what I have said, and repent in dust and ashes.** Job 42:1-6

The secret of much of our apparent success as adults seems to be exercising rational control over our world. But something funny happens on the way to the ultimate control we think we are about to gain—things fall apart. The center no longer holds. Our world spins out of control because the complexity of life makes absolute control impossible. Our inventiveness becomes our demon because we start more projects than we can finish, make more commitments than we can meet and crowd more and more activity into less and less time. We become prisoners of our own agenda. Our professional and personal relationships wear thin. Loneliness eats at us . . .Then unconscious hungers push their way into our awareness; cravings for love, for friendships, for mystery, for color and beauty and harmony—values not engineered by people trying to be masters of the universe, but rather gifts of grace.

Fr. Alfred McBride, O. Praem.
The Ten Commandments

Love As Jesus Loves

■ **Do unto others as you would have them do to you.**
Luke 6:31

Do you want to know the secret of true happiness? Of deep and genuine peace? Do you want to solve at a blow all your difficulties in relations with your neighbor, bring all polemic to an end, and avoid all dissension?

Well, decide here and now to love things and people as Jesus loved them, that is, to the point of self-sacrifice. Don't bother with the bookkeeping of love; love without keeping accounts. If you know someone who is decent and likeable, love him, but if someone else is very *un*likeable, love him just the same.

If someone greets you and smiles, greet him and smile back, but if someone else treads on your feet, smile just the same. If someone does you a good turn, thank the Lord for it, but if someone else slanders you, persecutes you, curses you, strikes you, thank him and carry on. Do not say, "I'm right and he's wrong." Say: "I must love him as myself." This is the kind of love Jesus taught: a love which transforms, vivifies, enriches, brings peace.

Carlo Carretto
Love Is For Living

Giving Ourselves

■ **"We have put aside everything to follow you."**
Mark 10:28

It is easy to measure our journey towards God in terms of how much we have given up. We can look back on our lives and see difficult choices we have made, decisions which may have involved turning away from family, or homeland or a hoped-for career. Surely, we tell ourselves, God will not forget our generosity, the price we paid for our discipleship. Like Peter, we can become defensive and begin to make claims.

Painful as it is to give up relationships, possessions and goals, it is even more painful to give up the self, to become so firmly rooted in God that we begin to lose the distinction as to where our lives end and God's begins. Giving up the self is the ultimate surrender, for it allows God to possess us fully. When we cling to our lives out of fear and the desire to control, then we are setting ourselves up as "gods." When we abandon every detail of our lives, then God can be God, and paradoxically, we can discover how rich it is to live in freedom and truth.

Elizabeth-Anne Vanek

Jesus, teach me to forget myself so that I may follow you more fully and freely.

Only God Is Enough

■ **You shall love the Lord, your God, with all your heart, with all your being, with all your strength, and with all your mind, and your neighbor as yourself.**

Luke 10:27

The experience of God and nothing short of that is the happiness of Christians. For although there is much besides to serve as subject of knowledge or motive for action or means of excitement, yet the affections require something more vast and more enduring that anything created . . .

God alone is sufficient for the heart who made it. I do not say, of course, that nothing short of the Creator can awaken and answer to our love, reverence and trust. People can do this for other people. People can be the object of love of others, and they can repay that love in kind. Indeed, it is a great duty, one of the two chief duties of religion, to be loving to our neighbor. But our hearts require something more permanent and uniform than other people can supply.

Cardinal John Henry Newman
Parochial and Plain Sermons

I will give thanks to the Lord with all my heart . . . God has won renown for wondrous deeds; gracious and merciful is the Lord.

Psalm 111:1, 4

We Need To Worship God

■ **Let us continually offer God a sacrifice of praise, that is, the fruit of lips that confess his name.**

Hebrews 13:15

God does not need praise, but we need to give it. Little girls at springtime often gather dandelions and give them to their mothers. Now the mothers do not need the dandelions. But the child needs to give them. By accepting the dandelions, the mother is training the child in love, kindness and obedience. Not to give a gift to the mother, however humble the gift, would mean the child was wanting in affection and obedience.

God does not need our praise, but we need to give it. God pretends to need us, but we really need Him for our perfection.

Bishop Fulton J. Sheen
Life Is Worth Living

God, may I recognize and fulfil my need to praise you each and every day of my life.

In Good Faith

■ O Lord, my heart is not proud, nor are my eyes haughty; I busy not myself with great things, nor with things too sublime for me. Nay rather, I have stilled and quieted my soul like a weaned child. Like a weaned child on its mother's lap. Psalm 131:1-2

How does one live fully in faith? How does one achieve the state of total dependence on God? The answer is simple: one doesn't achieve it at all; one receives it. It is not something acquired, like the skill of typing or the art of playing the piano. It is a gift from God; no one can give it to himself or herself.

We fail to depend on God whenever we depend too much on ourselves—our own ability, our own strength, our own determination. The realization of our utter dependence on God dawns on us only imperceptibly over a long period of time; it a gift that God reveals ever so slowly. All we can do is desire it and pray for the grace to grow less self-reliant and more and more dependent on the Lord.

Fr. John Catoir
Enjoy the Lord

O God, may I come more and more each day to rely on you rather than trying to rely too much on myself.

The Theology Of Prayer

■ **Ask and you shall receive; seek and you shall find; knock and it shall be opened to you.** Luke 11:9

The great theologian Richard Niebuhr was once asked, "What is your theology of prayer?" He replied, "I don't have a theology of prayer. Prayer is not something you talk about. **Prayer is something you do.** Prayer is not the consequence of theological thought. It is the basis for all theological thought."

Whatever prayer is—adoration, asking, telling, pleading, praising, interceding, confessing, thanking, or listening—it is between the human soul and God. It is a dynamic personal relationship between Creator and created. It is natural and normal, like breathing.

Anglican Archbishop Temple once said that when we pray, miracles occur. "Couldn't what you call 'miracles' be nothing but coincidence?" a skeptic asked. "Yes," said Temple, "but I have noticed that when I pray coincidences occur in my life, and when I don't pray the coincidences stop." Our lives are not mere incidents; they're "God-incidences" vitalized by prayer.

A. Philip Parham
Letting God

A God So Close

■ **In love God destined us for adoption through Jesus Christ.** Ephesians 1:4-5

The idea that God is an object outside of oneself to which one relates through prayer is totally unscriptural. It is heresy, and it should well be forgotten . . .

As Christians, the way we should look upon God is to see that we are in God and that God is in us. God is all around us and within us, so we can never escape the divine presence even if we wanted to. We are distinct from God but never totally apart from God. God and the true self are the same thing. We are not God in the absolute sense of being eternal and infinite, but we are God in the sense that the divine life is in us and we participate in the divine life. If we are seeking God through prayer and mysticism, the way to do so is to go through our innermost beings to the source, where God is dwelling.

Fr. Thomas Keating, O.C.S.O.
Speaking of Silence

In God, we live, move and have our being.
Acts 17:28

Seeing And Hearing

■ **While Jesus was speaking, a woman from the crowd called out, "Blest is the womb that bore you and the breast that nursed you!" "Rather," he replied, "blest are they who hear the word of God and keep it."**

Luke 11:27-28

Mary, what does it mean to believe that Christ rose from the dead? And did **you** see him during those days after his resurrection? Why don't the Gospels talk about you? You were the person most concerned. You were his mother! Why didn't he appear to **you**? [A slight, perhaps?]

Mary, was Jesus alluding to you when he said to Thomas, "Blessed are those who have not seen and yet believe"? (John 20:29) Perhaps you were the only one who did not need to see in order to believe . . . for you were blessed. I think that this was it.

And this is why you are our teacher in faith, and why Elizabeth's praise right at the beginning was the greatest praise: "Blessed are you who believed." **You did not need to see to believe.** You believed in your risen son, and that was enough for you. To believe in Jesus' resurrection means to believe without seeing.

Carlo Carretto
Blessed Are You Who Believed

'Do Not Disturb'

May God enlighten your innermost vision that you may know the great hope to which he has called you.

Ephesians 1:18

St. Teresa of Avila once wrote a list of inspirational thoughts to which she often referred to help her maintain peace of soul. Heading the list was, "Let nothing disturb you." It was as if she were trying to remind herself: "There will always be things going on about you that tend to disturb. You can't change that. But you are always free to choose whether or not you will allow them to rob you of your peace. You determine if things upset you."

Much of our unhappiness comes from our forgetting that we have the freedom to choose how we will respond to persons, events, circumstances. And because we forget, we allow our feelings of anger, impatience, uncharitableness to cloud our good sense and interfere with our making right choices. But the ability to choose the good is always there, as is God's grace.

Sr. Mary Terese Donze, A.S.C.

O Lord, help me to accept upsets in my life and offer them to you rather than fighting them.

What Matters Is Love

■ **In Christ Jesus neither circumcision nor the lack of it counts for anything; only faith, which expresses itself through love.** Galatians 5:6

What counts in love is to love. That is how it is here on earth. Love—supernatural love, which does not exclude natural love—is so simple and so complex. It requires that you do your part, and it awaits the other's part.

If you try to base your life on love, you will realize that it is worthwhile to do your part here on earth. You never know if you will be rewarded by the other. And it is not necessary that you should be. At times you will be disappointed, but you will never lose courage once you are convinced that what counts in love is to love.

Love Jesus in your neighbor, Jesus who always comes back to you, perhaps in other ways, not necessarily through that neighbor in that moment. He strengthens your soul against the hardships of the world, and fills it with love for all those who are close to you, as long as you bear in mind that what counts in love is to love.

Chiara Lubich
Meditations

Homebodies

■ **Like a bird that is far from its nest is a man who is far from his home.** Proverbs 27:8

Home is not a place; it is an attitude. It is an attitude which depends upon how much we are able to feel at home with ourselves as well as with others. Home is something which happens to a person; home-coming has less to do with geography than it has to do with a sense of personal integrity and inner wholeness. The most important of all endeavors in life is to come home. The most terrifying of fears is loneliness. It means that one has become a stranger to himself and, consequently, to others. To be lonely is to feel fear, to be forever unsettled, never at rest, in need of more reassurance than life can give. Someone truly loves us when he brings us home, when he makes us comfortable with ourselves, when he takes from us the strangeness we feel at being who we are. We are loved when we are no longer frightened with ourselves.

The human heart is made to be at home with itself. It is this aspiration which is at the heart of all yearning. We wish for home as our first wish, hope for home until our last hope, dream of home with every dream we form.

Anthony Padovano
Dawn Without Darkness

The Best Defense

When they bring you before synagogues, rulers and authorities, do not worry about how to defend yourselves or what to say. The Holy Spirit will teach you at that moment all that should be said. Luke 12:11

How much time we spend trying to defend and justify ourselves! Usually, the "authorities" we come up against are none other than family or friends or even ourselves. We would have a great deal more freedom and peace of mind if we could rely on the Holy Spirit to give us the words that needed to be said. We would probably say a lot less, too.

Does that mean we're more often wrong than not? Not necessarily. It's just that self-defense is useless—we very likely won't convince our adversary, and we won't wind up any more sure of ourselves than we started.

Justification really comes from the purity of our intentions and the strength of our love, something God knows much better than we do ourselves. We do our best when we can acknowledge our limits, accept God's help and then let go of the results.

Mark Neilsen

O God, give us this day the help we need to trust that the Holy Spirit will provide the defense we need.

Death's Door

■ **The Son of Man will come when you least expect him.** Luke 12:40

Death seems so monumental that surely we must be given some premonition of it. Surely God would not completely surprise us with something so important as the step into eternity! Surely death can't just happen in a micro-second, can't just pop out from behind a tree and declare, "I got ya!" Surely there will be time for preparation. Don't count on it.

That death can come unannounced like a thief, as Scripture warns, is a truly shocking realization. Yet if one prays each day and dwells daily with God—however briefly, it will not matter so much if death is a surprise. Daily prayer that unites us to God will take the shock and terror out of death because we will have an overpowering sense that we aren't facing it alone. God is at our side, and God will walk us through the gates of death when our time comes.

James E. Adams

Prayer is the best preparation for death because in it we are not only taken out of ourselves but also into the presence of God. Peter Kreeft

God's Great Love

■ **May you . . . know the love of Christ that surpasses knowledge.** Ephesians 3:19

Unbelievable. It seems unbelievable, yet it is gloriously true that God loves me!

Do I know that love? I may claim to know much about God's love, and yet I may not really experience that divine love personally. Jesus knew his Father's love better than anyone ever could. But in his earthly life, Jesus took time to nurture and relish that love every day even though he was extremely busy preaching to people and teaching the disciples.

We are often so busy with God's work that we neglect the God of work. Prayerful contact with God demands that we withdraw, as Jesus did, from the bustle of daily life. We need never fear that our human limitations are obstacles to God's Spirit working in us to make his love known to us and to transform us into bearers of his love. If we truly open our hearts in an effort to know God's love, we shall not be disappointed.

Sr. Peter Dupreé

Jesus, may I not just know the Father's love in the abstract but experience and feel it as well.

Jumping To Conclusions

■ **All depends on faith; everything is a grace.**

Romans 4:16

A minister held up a sign at the beginning of the sermon. It read: "GODISNOWHERE." He asked the congregation what it said and most responded, "GOD IS NOWHERE." Then the minister asked, "Didn't some of you see this message, 'GOD IS NOW HERE'?" Everyone did, of course, after being told.

What a true picture of our attitude about God! The same letter can carry a different message. It all depends on how we see it. We often believe God is absent. Less frequently we assume God is here with us. If we expect God to be away, God usually is away—for us. Yet if with hopeful expectation we feel sure of the divine presence, God's here! God is present as we expect that presence. We miss God when we jump to negative conclusions.

Life can be blessing or curse, problem or opportunity. It all depends on what we habitually look for: the good or the bad, God or no God at all. It's up to us. We have the choice of faith.

A. Philip Parham
Letting God

GODISNOWHERE

Our Duty To Share

■ Take care to guard against all greed, for though one may be rich, one's life does not consist of possessions.
Luke 12:15

Early Church Fathers as well as contemporary Popes have consistently said that it is a theft to keep what you do not need when others lack necessities. St. Basil put it graphically: **"The clothes in your closet that you no longer wear are clothes taken from the naked."** I am challenged by such statements to examine my own closet, and to give extra clothes and shoes to shelters serving the poor in my community.

But like most parents, I find a real tension here between putting away something for the kids' education and our retirement and responding to the immediate needs of others, especially the poor. There are no simple answers. Perhaps the best we can do is try to balance both these sets of legitimate concerns and to ask regularly what it is that we really need, in contrast with what are more like "wants."

Personal security— and national security as well— are ultimately not to be found in possessions. Loving relationships for individuals and cooperative relationships for nations are far more important. Let us use the possessions we have to share and build bridges with others.

James McGinnis

A Prayer About Praying

■ **Jesus asked him,"What do you want me to do for you?"** Mark 10:51

Lord, there are times when I feel I ask too much. One day I come to you with long lists of petitions, and the next I want you to extricate me from some impossible situation or to move mountains on my behalf. Often, I feel too needy: I am embarrassed by all the demands I place on you, that I don't simply sit in your presence and be still. Somehow, asking always seems the poorest kind of prayer . . .

And yet when blind Bartimaeus cried out to you in his need, you heard his voice above all the rest and asked him what he wanted; he spoke, and immediately received the gift of sight. This story gives me courage, Lord. It helps me to remember your compassion; it helps me to remember that you offer healing. Like Bartimaeus, I must learn to call out and name what it is I most desire. I deceive myself when I think you want to hear polite expressions of praise and gratitude, or when I treat you as some remote deity who will only incline a gracious ear if I use the right formulas. Rather, you want me to be myself, and even if I demand, argue and implore, you want to know what is in my heart.

Elizabeth-Anne Vanek

Unbounded Love

■ **You will be able to grasp fully, with all the holy ones, the breadth and length and height and depth of Christ's love, and experience this love which surpasses all knowledge, so that you may attain to the fullness of God.** Ephesians 3:18-19

Yes, we believe that God loves us, but deep within us we tend to harbor the feeling that we are not worthy of that love. We dwell on our human frailties, our constant transgressions. And we have a sneaking suspicion that the all-holy God could not possibly love someone like us.

True, it is good to acknowledge and face our infidelities. But God would far rather we look not so much at ourselves, but at him and his tremendous love. And what marvelous proofs we have of this love!

God chose not only to create each of us as individuals, calling us by name, but to include each of us in the stupendous Plan of Salvation. God gave each one of us our specific role in the world, the gifts to fulfill that role and grace without limit to help us be faithful.

Once we fully accept the glorious fact of God's unbounded love for each of us as individuals, we will respond by trying to be worthy of such love and thereby prove our love for God.

Sr. Peter Dupreé

How Much Is Much?

■ **Much will be required of the person entrusted with much, and still more will be demanded of the person entrusted with more.** Luke 12:48

When we hear those words, do we always think of others who are really "wealthy?" Do we say, "Yes, if I had 'much,' I would be generous." We never seem to realize that most of us indeed have "much," perhaps not always in material goods but in other blessings of time and talent.

Do we excuse ourselves too easily from sharing those? Can we justify some of the luxuries we call necessities when even one person is in want and we have not helped that person?

It may be well to reexamine the question of "much" in our own circumstances. Our God is a just God who knows our hearts. Can you visualize God saying, "I gave you much. What are you doing with it?" Think of this and tremble. But do not become despairing either. Our God is a merciful God who gives even when we have not yet learned to.

Joan Zrilich

O Lord, help me to be generous with the "much" you have given me.

Boatmanship

■ **As slaves of Christ, do the will of God from the heart, willingly serving the Lord and not human beings.** Ephesians 6:6-7

Someone once observed that disciples come in three varieties; tugboats, sailboats and rafts.

Tugboats follow Jesus not only in sunny weather but also in stormy weather. They follow him not only when the wind and the waves serve them but also when they oppose them. They are people who love not only when they feel like it but always, day in, day out.

Sailboat disciples follow Jesus only in sunny weather. They go in his direction only when the wind and the waves serve them. When stormy weather comes, they tend to go in the direction they are blown. They follow the crowd more than they follow Jesus.

Finally, there are raft disciples. They are not really followers of Jesus at all. They won't even follow him when the wind and the waves serve them. They go in his direction only when they are pulled or pushed. They act like Christians because they have to or because it is to their personal advantage to do so.

Fr. Mark Link, S.J.
Decision

'Peter Pan' Christians

■ **Let us, then, be children no longer, tossed here and there, carried about by every wind of doctrine that originates in human trickery and skill in proposing error. Rather, let us profess to the truth in love and grow to the full maturity of Christ the head.**

Ephesians 4:14-15

All too often believers have envisioned God as a wimp. The contemporary version of the wimp is the limp, value-free God who loves us vaguely and makes no demands upon us. This is the God of the eternal adolescent who is willing forever to search and never to find and who refuses to make decisions and commitments. **This is the God of the Peter Pans who dread the thought of growing up.** Such people like the Jesus of the open road but block out the Christ who firmly sets his face toward Jerusalem with its promise of sacrifice and redemptive pain.

The real God is not a wimp. God sympathizes with our weaknesses but offers us inner strength. God knows we face trials, but tolerates our failures if we have the good sense and the guts to turn them into stepping-stones to virtue.

Fr. Alfred McBride, O.Praem.
The Ten Commandments

A Prayer Of Listening

■ **You shall love the Lord your God with your whole heart.** Matthew 22:37

I am listening, Lord. I have finally banished all distractions and unwanted images. I have finally stopped fidgeting and wriggling, both symptoms of struggle. I am no longer staring at book titles or smears on window panes. Nor am I wrapped up in the torrents of words which too often consume my time with you—those lists of people whom I want to remember, things for which I am grateful, petitions for the suffering world. I am still, within and without.

In this silence, in this stillness, I wait to hear your voice, Lord. I have told you so often about my desire to serve. I have offered you my gifts, time and time again, hoping you find them acceptable. I want to be commissioned for some glorious task, to pour myself out that others may come and find you. But it is always the same: the only words I hear are softer than the beat of my heart. "You are the gift," you say. "I want your love—nothing more."

Elizabeth-Anne Vanek

We Are Always Thirsty

■ **My soul is thirsting for the living God.** Psalm 42:3

When Jesus told the woman at the well that whoever drank of him would never again know thirst, he had her attention immediately. No matter how much water she would draw each day she would always have to return for more because thirst returned.

Though water is more accessible twenty centuries later, thirst still demands to be slaked. The writer Thomas Dubay points out graphically that we not only thirst (verb), we are thirsty (adjective), but are actually a living thirst (noun). Every choice we make, day in and day out, proves this to us. We seek, we desire, we want, we lack. Nothing is ever enough. We are incarnated thirsts. We yearn for endless love, endless delight, endless security, endless happiness. We are always thirsty with a thirst that nothing finite can ever quench.

Sr. Charleen Hug, S.N.D.

My soul is thirsting for the living God.
Psalm 42

Reaching For Happiness

■ **Happy the one who finds wisdom, who gains understanding.** Proverbs 3:13

We are made for happiness and there is nothing wrong in reaching out for it. Unfortunately, most of us are so deprived of happiness that as soon as it comes along, we reach out for it with all our strength and try to hang on to it for dear life. That is a mistake. The best way to receive it is to give it away. If you give everything back to God, you will always be empty, and when you are empty, there is more room for God.

The experience of God usually comes as something you feel you have experienced before. God is so well suited to us that any experience of God is a feeling of completion or well-being. What was lacking in us seems to be somehow mysteriously restored. This experience awakens confidence, peace, joy and reverence all at the same time. Of course, the next thing that occurs to us is, "This is great! How am I going to hang on to it?" That's normal. But experience teaches that that is exactly the worst thing to do. The innate tendency to hang on, to possess, is the biggest obstacle to union with God.

Fr. Thomas Keating, O.C.S.O.
Open Mind, Open Heart

Daily Conversion

■ **I acknowledged my sin to you, my guilt I covered not. I said, "I confess my faults to the Lord," and you took away the guilt of my sin.** Psalm 32:5

Jesus, we are called to conversion every day of our life; we are called to call others to conversion, for as long as we live. Our first task is with ourselves. It is easy to slip into faults that tend to grow and even overwhelm us. We can ignore them,we can be blind to our own sins, we can become too lazy to reform and truly get rid of the faults we have.

Teach us, Jesus, to be converted to You, day by day. Help us to realize the joy that You have, when You know that we are seriously trying to reform, to get rid of our sins, and be totally converted to Your way of loving and living.

Fr. Killian Speckner
The Prayers of Father Killian

Realizing Our Potential

■ **Dearly beloved, we are God's children now.**

1 John 3:2

If we look at the Church's calendar of saints, we see fishermen and farmers, husbands and wives, rich and poor, soldiers and scholars, even kings and queens honored there. Everyone is called to achieve his or her fullest potential, to be a truly whole and holy person, regardless of occupation or state of life. . . All the saints and mystics have a holistic outlook on life that is refreshing. They see themselves for what they are and invite God to make them all they can be.

This holistic spirituality is rewarding but also demanding. **Catholic holiness is not a Jesus-and-me attitude. It is not enough to go to church on Sunday and leave the rest of your life unchanged.** True holiness requires conversion of the whole person, a transformation of the total personality. And it requires a conversion of your life-style, no matter where you live or what you do for a living.

Fr. Richard Rohr, O.F.M. & Joseph Martos
Why Be Catholic?

O God, help me to give myself to you wholely and freely so that you can make me holy.

Remembering The Dead

■ **For if he were not expecting the fallen to rise again, it would have been useless and foolish to pray for them in death.** 2 Maccabees 12:44

Let us remember our departed dear ones. Names, persons, faces and kind words come back to our minds, filling them with the memory of days past in their company, of places animated by their wonderful and loving presence. The great saints, too, lived through the agony of these separations. St. Augustine describes the suffering he endured at the death of his mother. "As I closed her eyes an immense sadness pressed heavily on my heart and became a flood of tears. But what was it then which hurt me so terribly within if not the raw wound caused by the sudden breakup of our sweet and dear life together to which we had grown so accustomed?" If the saints can feel such separations so deeply that their hearts break, can things be any different for us? But the great saints also show us the way which has been opened before us when confronted with the mystery of death. It is the way of Christ's Passover, Christ who by his death has destroyed our death and by his Resurrection has given us the gift of life. So we remember our departed ones also in the gladness of Christ's resurrection.

Cardinal Carlo M. Martini, S.J.
Journeying with the Lord

A Welcome Sign

■ **Rejoice with me because I have found my lost sheep.** Luke 15:6

In a short story called "Somebody's Son," Richard Pindell tells of a runaway boy named David, who is writing a letter to his mother. He expresses hope that his old-fashioned father would forgive him and accept him again as a son. The boy is hesitant, however, and asks for a signal. "If Dad will take me back," he wrote, "ask him to tie a white cloth on the apple tree in the field next to our house."

Days later David is on a train which is rapidly approaching his house. Soon the apple tree will be in sight. But David can't bring himself to look for it. He is afraid the white cloth won't be there. Turning to a man sitting next to him, he asks the stranger to watch for the tree and the white cloth.

As the train rumbles past the tree, David stares straight ahead, and in a quaking voice asks, "Mister, is a white cloth tied to one of the branches?"

In a surprised voice, the man says, "Why son, there's a white cloth tied to practically every branch!"

Fr. Mark Link, S.J.
Decision

Rewarding Relationships

■ **For the gifts and the call of God are irrevocable.**
Romans 11:29

If we had our lives to live over again, 63 percent of us who are parents would have the same number of children as we do now, according to a recent Parents magazine survey. But 26 percent of us would have more and, among the childless, 73 percent would have children.

This means, says a sociologist, that we **"feel that those relationships which demand the most accountability, the greatest amount of intimacy, and the greatest investment of time and energy are also the ones that are the most rewarding."**

We are called to the same kind of relationship with God—and it clearly can be a relationship that is even more profoundly rewarding than those of family. We are drawn to a closeness with one who knows us better than we know ourselves and, each day, we are invited to learn more about God. We are held accountable to pursue a relationship with God and to devote much time and energy to it—to pray always.

Saying yes to God's call makes the good times better and the rough times easier.

Charlotte Rancilio

Turning A New Leaf

■ **Your attitude must be like that of Christ: though he was in the form of God he did not deem equality with God something to be grasped at.** Philippians 2:5-6

One tree in our neighborhood never seems to let go of its fall foliage. Long after the golds and reds have carpeted the lawns, this one tree holds onto its leaves tenaciously, as if to boast, "I am tree, I do not change."

It is a healthy reminder for me that change is an important part of life, and needs to be accepted. When Jesus taught, the Pharisees criticized his words because their image of God was narrow and pride-filled. They refused to change. To accept the words of Jesus would have meant letting go of their way of thinking, and no longer "grasping at" their image of God. It would have meant a change in attitude.

The curled leaves on the tree remind me to let go of my narrow views of other people, to look at them through Jesus' eyes, and to open my heart to the wind of the Spirit whose freeing touch will change my heart.

Lucia Godwin

Open-Heartedness

■ **He said to them, "Whenever you give a lunch or dinner, do not invite your friends, or brothers or relatives or wealthy neighbors. They might invite you in return, and thus repay you. No, when you have a reception invite beggars, and the crippled, the lame and the blind."** Luke 14:12-13

During Jesus' public ministry he had no home. He often stayed with different people on his journeys. Hospitality was freely given in this desert culture, and no payment was expected of the guest. However, Jesus is suggesting the hosts open their homes to the dregs of society, the beggars, the broken, the blind. Physical weakness and brokenness were thought to be a scourge from God because of sin. Jesus is telling his host to accept the socially unacceptable.

It is easy to open our hearts and homes to those who think alike and who share the same family or background, but we are encouraged by Jesus to invite those who are different from us into our lives, whether the difference is caused by economics, race, religion or social standing. We then begin to see others as Jesus sees them and are enabled to love them because God loved them first.

Lucia Godwin

Seeds Of Faith

■ **If you had faith the size of a mustard seed, you could say to this sycamore, "Be uprooted and transplanted into the sea," and it would obey you.** Luke 17:6

How small and apparently powerless is a seed, especially a mustard seed. Yet most of us have experienced the determination of a seed to grow, to push its way through the soil. Broken rocks and sidewalks are evidence of this.

How much more powerful must be the seed of faith within us. Do we experience its power to break through the concrete that blocks growth in our lives? No one tells the seed it cannot be done. It just relies on its inner striving for life. We have that innate instinct for life, which is God within us. We have the advantage of consciousness to lead us in a certain direction. There are sycamores in our own lives and in our world. The power of our faith can move them. All that is needed is for us to give the command.

Sr. Ancilla Keinberger, O.P.

Duty-Bound

■ **We have done no more than our duty.** Luke 17:10

The word duty may have a servile ring to it; visions of slaves and soldiers; the inferior taking orders from the superior. But duty doesn't have to be something imposed on us from outside. Within us all is the sense of right and wrong, a truth that burns in our hearts. Our duty is simply being true to ourselves, to the God within, and to the circumstances of our lives.

In most of our everyday experiences we know what we must do. We know what we must do in family relationships, work situations, and in the broader scope of our lives. We may not call it duty, but our own inner integrity demands a response. This is our duty. Others may praise us, deride us, or simply ignore us. They may misunderstand our sense of duty.

We may not be hailed as heroes or heroines, but we will be able to claim the peace and fulfillment that comes with a free commitment to our duty. And that is no small claim.

Sr. Ancilla Keinberger, O.P.

Jesus, help me to tend to my most important duties faithfully and lovingly.

Praising God Always

■ **Give thanks in all circumstances.**

1 Thessalonians 5:18

I have a tendency to ask for help only when I am in need and to live as if I can handle life by myself most of the time. Occasionally I say "thank you" to people or to God, but mostly I forget about my basic dependence and act with the illusion of self-control.

A life of faith is a life of gratitude—it means a life in which I am willing to experience my complete dependence upon God at all times, and to praise and give thanks to my Creator unceasingly for the gift of being. A truly eucharistic life means always saying thanks to God, always praising God, and always being more surprised by the abundance of God's goodness and love.

Fr. Henri J.M. Nouwen
The Road to Daybreak

The Lord gives and the Lord . . . gives some more. Blessed be the name of the Lord!

Our Real Needs

■ **My God in turn will supply your needs fully in a way worthy of his magnificent riches in Christ Jesus.**

Philippians 4:19

A real gift in today's consumer society is being capable of distinguishing between wants and needs. Happy the person who possesses this gift. Strong convictions alone are no guarantee that our time, energy, money, love will be expended this day in pursuit of our needs instead of our wants. **So clear a vision can be obtained only by living the gospel.**

But if we live by the gospel, then we must live for our neighbor as well as for ourselves. And if we live for our neighbor, we must attend to his or her needs. What if one day, just for today, every committed Christian were dedicated to supplying and fulfilling the needs of others? This is no mere ideal; for Christians, this is our challenge. What's in it for us? St. Paul says: "My God in turn will supply your needs fully in a way worthy of his magnificent riches in Christ Jesus."

Sr. Mary Charleen Hug, S.N.D.

Hoping Against Hope

■ **God is not the God of the dead but of the living. All are alive for God.** Luke 20:38

Why should I cherish a hope that devours me—the hope for perfect happiness in this life—when such hope, doomed to frustration, is nothing but despair?

My hope is in what the eye has never seen. So let me not trust in visible rewards. My hope is in what the human heart cannot feel. So let me not trust in the feelings of my heart. My hope is in what the human hand has never touched. Do not let me trust what I can grasp between my fingers. Death will loosen my grasp and my vain hope will be gone.

Let my trust be in your mercy, O God, not in myself. Let my hope be in your love, not in health or strength or ability or human resources. If I trust you, everything else will become, for me, strength, health and support. Everything will bring me to heaven. If I do not trust you, everything will be my destruction.

Thomas Merton
Thoughts in Solitude

Pray All Day

■ **Jesus told his disciples a parable on the necessity of praying always and not losing heart . . .** Luke 18:1

A short, active prayer can help you deal with many daily stresses. It involves silently repeating a short phrase from the Scriptures, six to ten syllables in length, over and over . . . "O God, come to my assistance!" "Not my will but yours be done." "Praise God, O my soul!"

Some of you will think, "Monks have nothing else to do all day long but say these silly prayers, but what about us, who have to earn a living and raise a family?" All I can say is, you need to pray more than we do! You don't always have supportive structures to remind you of the spiritual values of life. Although you may have established a reservoir of interior silence and prayer earlier in the day, once you hit the street, the water starts to drain out fast. But suppose you were saying an active prayer over and over to yourself. I'll bet there are several hours in every day when you could be doing this: while you are doing chores, taking a shower, changing diapers . . . you could be silently working your prayer into your unconscious . . . knocking on God's door.

Fr. Thomas Keating, O.C.S.O
Speaking of Silence

Heavenly Hope

■ **The grace of God has appeared, offering salvation to all. It trains us to reject godless ways and worldly desires, and live temperately, justly and devoutly in this age as we await our blessed hope, the appearing of the glory of the great God and of our Savior Christ Jesus.** Titus 2:11-13

There is a story of a woman who had been used to every luxury and to all respect. She died, and when she arrived in heaven, an angel was sent to conduct her to her house there. They passed many a lovely mansion and the woman thought that each one, as they came to it, must be the one allotted to her. When they had passed through the main streets they came to the outskirts where the houses were much smaller; and on the very fringe they came to a house which was little more than a shack.

"This is your house," said the angel.

"What!" said the woman. "I cannot live in that."

"I am sorry," said the angel, "but that is all we could build for you with the materials you sent up."

Fr. Brian Cavanaugh, T.O.R.
The Sower's Seeds

Gratefulness

■ **Jesus took the occasion to say, "Were not all ten made whole? Where are the other nine?"** Luke 17:17

What has become of gratitude? Jesus questioned the lack of appreciation of the nine who had been healed. How often have we given or received gratitude? With the many things we have to do, expressing gratitude may be overlooked. We may put it off and then forget or we may assume the other person knows we are grateful. How many "thank you" notes or phone calls are postponed indefinitely?

Problems and difficulties are part of our lives. There are periods of sorrow when gratitude isn't experienced. But maybe there has been a time of fullness where we felt just great and gratitude came easily. Gratefulness needs to be expressed, for it enriches the giver as well as the receiver. It opens one up to the possibilities and positive values in life.

Amid our daily problems, can we recognize moments of grace and healing? Can we, right now, think of a reason to be grateful? Let us do ourselves and the world a favor by expressing gratitude this day.

Sr. Ancilla Keinberger, O.P.

No Secrets In Prayer

■ **O God, be merciful to me a sinner.** Luke 18:13

We need a very holistic view of prayer. A view of prayer that pulls us away from our intellectualizing practices, in which God becomes one of the many problems we have to address. Real prayer penetrates to the marrow of our soul and leaves nothing untouched.

The prayer of the heart is the prayer that does not allow us to limit our relationship with God to interesting words or pious emotions. By its very nature such prayer transforms our whole being into Christ precisely because it opens the eyes of our soul to the truth of ourselves as well as to the truth of God. In our heart we come to see ourselves as sinners embraced by the mercy of God. It is this vision that makes us cry out, "Lord Jesus Christ, Son of the Living God, have mercy on me, a sinner."

The prayer of the heart challenges us to hide absolutely nothing from God and to surrender ourselves unconditionally to divine mercy.

Fr. Henri J.M. Nouwen
The Way of the Heart

O God, have mercy on me, a sinner.

Simplify Your Heart

■ **Unless you turn and become like children, you will not enter the kingdom of heaven.** Matthew 18:3

Dear Child: I want you to simplify your heart. I want you to take small steps. I want you to do only one thing at a time. I want you to be as single-hearted as a child.

Reduce your days to moments—small bunches of time. Approach each piece of time in wonder and trust. Consecrate it to me wholeheartedly and then open the package to see what is contained within it. Then, go on to the next.

Pray one prayer at a time. Do an act of love for one person at a time. Talk to one person and give that person your whole attention and love. Face one problem at a time. Consider it deeply. Give it to me in prayer. Do what you decide, then leave it in my hands. Do not pick it up again.

There is a time for grieving, a time for rest, a time for laughing, a time for tears, a time for work, a time for travel, a time for action—but not all at once!

Be childlike in your approach. Trust me like a child. Love everyone you meet like a child. Shake off discouragement like a child. Put your hand in mine and walk joyfully with me.

Kelly B. Kelly
Grains of Wheat

Food For Thoughts

■ **For everything created by God is good, and nothing is to be rejected when received with thanksgiving, for it is made holy by the invocation of God in prayer.**

1 Timothy 4:4-5

What counts are not our prayers but our prayer, not our prayerfulness but the forms by which we express and sustain it. How easily we slide into thinking of our prayers as the "real" prayer. . . Rightly understood, our prayers at table will be an expression of thankfulness and a reminder to eat every bite of this meal thankfully. Gratefulness will turn the whole meal into prayer, for after we pray our prayers, we will pray our soup, salad, and dessert, and then pray another set prayer at the end as a reminder to continue to pray even after the meal.

When we get the relationship of prayers to prayer confused, we begin to think that truly prayerful people can be recognized by longer and more frequent prayers. This would be like thinking that the best car is the one that uses the most fuel. In fact, a good case could be made for the claim that spiritual athletes get more mileage out of few prayers. It is not prayers that count, but prayerfulness . . . Prayer is grateful living.

Br. David Steindl-Rast, O.S.B.
Gratefulness—The Heart of Prayer

Prayer Of Suffering

■ **By patient endurance you will save your lives.**
Luke 21:19

When suffering comes to you (and sooner or later it comes to everyone) don't look or search for any special method of prayer. Just be. Just sit and accept your cross; accept it totally into the depths of your being. How easily I say this but how terribly anguishing is this prayer—and how terribly powerful!

Remember that you need not words or thoughts. This prayer is a silent acceptance of the suffering of your life. That suffering may be sickness or rejection or separation from a loved one, or loneliness or failure or loss of reputation or misunderstanding or fear of death. Or it may be existential dread—the suffering of separated being. Whatever it is, sit with it. Don't run away. Don't try to escape. Don't fight. Sit with your cross.

Fr. William Johnston, S.J.
Being in Love

Underjoyed

■ **God is not the God of the dead but of the living, for to God all are alive.** Luke 20:38

To be redeemed in the blood of Christ and to be offered the promise of eternal life is part of the total Christian experience. Why then are we not joyful in our daily life? Instead of singing with joy and thanksgiving, we often become discouraged and seem to assume a posture of resignation. We think the worst, and this is a distortion of the truth. Only God has the whole picture and only faith can lift us out of our own dark interpretation of human events.

Life is a splendid, glorious adventure. The shadows are there and they have their purpose. Because of them we are more ready to treasure the rays of golden sunshine. They must be seen in context. The resurrection of Jesus was preceded by pain. As terrible as that pain was, it was a saving pain; it was the coin that purchased our redemption. God draws good from evil and we need only trust that God will do the same in our lives. God is at work in each life, writing straight with crooked lines, bringing us to glory and happiness. The dominant theme of life is hopeful, full of promise, and for this we are grateful.

Fr. John Catoir
Enjoy the Lord

Seeing In The Dark

■ **Lord, please let me see.** Luke 18:41

I once knew a sister who had gone blind as a consequence of diabetes. She could be found moving fairly easily through the Motherhouse she knew so well; and her sisters seemed sensitive to the balance between the help she genuinely needed and the independence she desired. When I learned of her death some years ago, I couldn't help but wonder at the great joy when her heart met God and her sight was restored.

Life sometimes leads us into periods of darkness. We search for understanding where we once were so certain; stumble where we once walked with ease. The landmarks of our lives may still dot the landscape, but now they confuse where they once reassured.

Such times invite us to trust that we are companioned in the darkness, that the darkness is meant to empty us of our certainties, our way of seeing things. Eventually, if we but wait faithfully by the side of the road, we will discover that Jesus has been beside us all along, that our plea to see again has been met with the call to see with new eyes, God's eyes.

Sharon T. Santia

'The Great Amen'

■ **They throw down their crowns before the throne and sing: "O Lord our God, you are worthy to receive glory and honor and power! For you have created all things; by your will they came to be and were made!"**

Revelation 4:10-11

As the final word of my prayer drifts away, I listen for the Great Amen. Like thunder it comes rolling back. Or it leaps across the roofs, racing through the tree leaves, whipping wildly over electrical wires, and with the surge of a cosmic-sea wave it crashes on my shore: "Amen."

From all creation comes the chorus, from snow-swept glaciers and ever-extending deserts, from dark-brown jungle rivers and majestic mountain ranges, from vast redwood forests and endless rolling prairies, from flocks of flying birds and herds of wild animals, from swarms of monarch butterflies and schools of fish in the ocean deep; to each of my prayers comes the Great Amen.

From God's great family, one and all, rainbow-colored in skin and faith, from those of every compass point, from country, town and urban slum, it comes, it always comes. From angels and archangels, saints and mystics all, it slowly swells, then rushes into the cave of my heart: "AMEN, AMEN, AMEN."

Fr. Edward Hays
Prayers for a Planetary Pilgrim

Piece Of The Rock

■ **Say among the nations, "Yahweh is our Rock!"**
Psalm 96:10

How is God like a rock? Rock is heavy, massive and hard. It stands for might and dependability. When we stand in a canyon before a huge wall of rock, rest on a slab of granite or clamber over rocks pounded by ocean waves, we sense a quiet strength . . .

This is God for us; the rock bottom of the universe. God is always there, steady and silent, inscrutable and invariable. God is the solid Spirit that supports all, the rock of ages.

Happy are those who have God as the rock of their life. These are the people who acknowledge their dependence on God, make God the center of gravity and the source for help. They are upheld by the assurance of God's deep and lasting love for them. Their world may fall apart, yet they stand firm. People may turn against them, criticize them, threaten them, and attack them, yet they remain calm. Their plans and projects may disintegrate, but they do not despair.

Sr. Mary Kathleen Glavich, S.N.
Voices: Messages in Gospel Symbols

A Psalm Of Thanksgiving

O God, show your faithfulness, bless us,
and make your face smile on us!
For then the earth will acknowledge your ways,
and all nations will know of your power to save.
May all the nations praise you, O God;
may all the nations praise you!
Let the nations shout and sing for joy
since you dispense true justice to the world.
You grant strict justice to the peoples;
on earth you guide the nations.
Let the nations praise you, God;
let all the nations praise you!
The soil has given its harvest;
God, our God, has blessed us.
May God continue to bless us;
and let God be feared to the very ends of the earth.

Psalm 67

Path To Peace

■ **If only you had known the path to peace this day; but you have completely lost it from view!** Luke 19:42

God desires our happiness, insofar as it is possible, and not merely that we be "content." We often confuse happiness with contentment. Happiness has a profoundly human, spiritual and moral character. It means an interior plentitude. We can be happy amid suffering, physical evil, scarcity and when our earthly expectations fail to materialize.

Contentment comes through pleasure and the satisfaction of immediate temporal goals. Contentment is of short duration and cannot give us fulfillment. Too many people seek contentment and not happiness. **Worse yet, too many people are not even interested in true happiness**, which always requires moral and spiritual progress, and prefer to live in the pursuit of a spurious contentment.

True happiness is like true freedom and authentic liberation. Few people want to be freed, and few people want true liberation, to be the protagonists of their own lives. Many prefer to live with the security and contentment that is as false as it is enslaving.

Fr. Segundo Galilea
The Music of God

The Meaning Of Life

■ **Enter God's gates with thanksgiving, and the courts with praise! Give thanks to God; bless God's name! For Yahweh is good; God's steadfast love endures forever, and God's faithfulness to all generations.** Psalm 100:4-5

We humans cannot find peace of heart unless we find meaning in life. Meaning is that in which our hearts find rest. We never achieve meaning as one achieves a purpose, by hard work. It is always received as pure gift. And yet we must *give* meaning to our lives. How can we do this? Through gratefulness. Gratefulness is the inner gesture of *giving* meaning to our life by *receiving* life as a gift. The deepest meaning of any given moment lives in the fact that it is given. Gratefulness recognizes, acknowledges and celebrates this meaning.

Br. David Steindl-Rast, O.S.B.
Gratefulness—The Heart of Prayer

No one can be unhappy and grateful at the same time. Anthony de Mello

Good Eggs And Bad

■ I saw a new heaven and a new earth. The former heavens and the former earth had passed away.
Revelation 21:1

Christ says, "Give me all. I don't want so much of your time and so much of your money and so much of your work: I want you. I have not come to torment your natural self, but to kill it. No half-measures are any good. I don't want to cut off a branch here and a branch there, I want to have the whole tree down . . . Hand over the whole natural self, all the desires which you think innocent as well as the ones you think wicked—the whole outfit.I will give you a new self. In fact, I will give you Myself—my own will shall become yours."

. . . We must go in for the full treatment. It is hard; but the sort of compromise we are all hankering after is harder—in fact, it is impossible. It may be hard for an egg to turn into a bird; it would be a jolly sight harder for it to learn to fly while remaining an egg. We are like eggs at present. And you cannot go on indefinitely being just an ordinary, decent egg. We must be hatched or go bad.

C.S. Lewis
The Joyful Christian

The Eleventh Hour

■ **The day I speak of will come upon all who dwell on the face of the earth. So be on the watch. Pray constantly for the strength to escape whatever is in prospect, and to stand secure before the Son of Man.**

Luke 21:35-36

Shall we obtain the grace to make our last conscious moment of human life a moment filled with the prayer of decision? Such a prayer will lift up all that we were and are, all that we have done and suffered, in oblation to the mercy of God. As the shades of death darken in our minds, shall we turn a last glance of faith on him who has crossed the bar of death and yet lives? Shall we say to him at that moment,"Come, Lord Jesus"? Shall we be able to pray in that hour of decision, to commend our souls into the hands of God? May God mercifully grant us the grace to depart from this world in prayer, so that the last thought in our minds may fit us for life everlasting. Blessed is the person who can utter a prayer of decision when the most decisive hour comes . . .

That prayer of decision that we wish to say in the hour of our death must be said by us again and again in our life. We must pray now for the grace of fortitude.

Fr. Karl Rahner, S.J.
Words of Faith

A Grateful Heart

One of them, realizing that he had been cured, came back praising God in a loud voice. He threw himself on his face at the feet of Jesus and spoke his praises.
Luke 17:15-16

Gratitude is more than mental exercise, more than a formula of words. We cannot be satisfied to make a mental note of things which God has done for us and then perfunctorily thank God for favors received.

To be grateful is to recognize the love of God in everything God has given us—and God has given us everything. Every breath we draw is a gift of divine love, every moment of existence is a grace, for it brings with it immense graces from God. Gratitude therefore takes nothing for granted, is never unresponsive, is constantly awakening to new wonder and to praise of the goodness of God. **For the grateful person knows that God is good, not by hearsay but by experience.** That makes all the difference.

Thomas Merton
Thoughts in Solitude

Wonderfully Made

■ **How great and wonderful are all your works . . . who would not revere and praise your name, O Lord?**
Revelation 15:3-4

Many things remind us that God's works are great and wonderful: the marvelous vistas of nature, the wonder of birth, the richness of human language and creativity can all stir the heart to praise God.

Perhaps, though, for all that we might rejoice in the wonders of creation and the richness and generosity of the Creator, we sometimes fail to include our own lives in the list of God's great and wonderful works. Yet the shape of my heart did not escape God's notice nor form outside God's loving labor. Nor, once formed, was I set adrift from the Creator's love and care.

Yes, the twists and turns of life, a sense of our shortcomings and failings can blind us to the dignity we possess simply by virtue of the gift of life. Yet, numbered as we are among God's wonderful works, each one of us has cause to revere and praise the name of God.

Sharon T. Santia

O God, praised be your name now and forever—on earth and in heaven. Amen!

Trust Anew

■ **Neither must you be perturbed when you hear of wars and insurrections. These things are bound to happen first, but the end does not follow immediately.**

Luke 21:9

When we look at the world around us today, it is easy to become discouraged and depressed like the people to whom Jesus was speaking in today's Gospel. Wars, insurrections, plagues, and famines continue to occur. Sometimes the tragedies of our personal lives—illness, death of loved ones, unemployment—weigh us down with sorrow and despair. "How," we may cry out, "can we avoid becoming 'perturbed'?"

In the turmoil of times like these we can come to recognize the permanent, unchanging truth of God's love and care for us all. But first, we must be willing to let go of our old ways of thinking and acting, to grow and to change. In these last days of the Church year, we begin to look forward to Advent and the coming of Jesus Christ into our lives anew. Let us try to place our trust in our loving God and pray for the patience and courage to continue working for necessary changes both in the world and in our own lives.

Mary H. Rea

Sense Of Wonder

■ **No ear has ever heard, no eye ever seen, any God but you doing such deeds for those who wait for him.**
Isaiah 64:3

The final weeks of the liturgical year are traditionally the time of thinking of the last things, of the end of time. But before I can contemplate the end I have to think about the beginning, and no one is very certain about the beginning, that moment when God created the universe out of sheer *joie de vivre*. There are several conflicting theories of the creation of the universe . . . but none of these theories answers the question of why there's anything at all. *Why isn't there just nothing?*

My children asked me these things and I was hard put to answer their questions. Why is there anything? Well, God made something out of nothing. Why? Didn't God like nothing? Well, God is love, and it is the nature of love to create . . .

Madeleine L'Engle
The Irrational Season

Alleluia! Oh, give thanks for God is good. God's faithful love endures forever! Who can recount the mighty deeds of God, or proclaim adequate praise? Psalm 106:1-2

An Advent Reading

The Lord is waiting to show you favor, and he rises to pity you;

For the Lord is a God of justice; blessed are all who wait for him!

O People of Zion, who dwell in Jerusalem, no more will you weep.

He will be gracious to you when you cry out, as soon as he hears he will answer you.

The Lord will give you the bread you need and the water for which you thirst.

No longer will your Teacher hide himself, but with your own eyes you shall see your Teacher,

While from behind, a voice shall sound in your ears: "This is the way; walk in it," when you would turn to the right or to the left.

And you shall consider unclean your silver-plated idols and your gold-covered images;

You shall throw them away like filthy rags to which you say, "Begone!"

Isaiah 30:18-22

Paying Attention

■ **Be on guard lest your spirits become bloated with indulgence and drunkenness and worldly cares . . . So be on the watch. Pray constantly . . .** Luke 21:34, 36

Meditation summons us to open our hearts to the light and life of Christ by the very simple expedient of paying attention; that is, paying attention to their presence within us. We pay attention to our own true nature, and by becoming fully conscious of the union of our nature with Christ, we become fully ourselves. **By becoming fully ourselves we enter the fullness of life Jesus has brought us.** We come to appreciate in the reverent silence of our prayer, that we are infinitely holy as temples of God's own Spirit. We learn to remember who we are, and that our vocation is to look upon and contemplate the Godhead itself and thus to be ourselves divinized. As one of the Eucharistic prayers expresses it, "On that day we shall see You our God as You are and we shall become like You." The great masters of prayer in the Christian tradition have all understood prayer in this way—as a discovery of self that takes us far beyond narrow self-consciousness.

Fr. John Main, O.S.B.
Word Into Silence

All Need Prayer

■ **All have sinned and fall short of the glory of God.**
Romans 3:23

The famous evangelist Billy Sunday always made it a practice to pray for specific people in each city he was to preach in. Before going to one city, he wrote his usual letter to the mayor asking for names of those in need of special prayers. The mayor responded by sending him the city directory! Nothing could be truer—we all need prayer.

When we pray, what happens? Usually our mood changes. Our thoughts focus on God. One thing is true for a sincere prayer: it is practically impossible to pray for someone and also hate at the same time. If resentment and ill will rise up in us, we stop praying.

If we approach God in humble petition and in earnest concern for ourselves or others, our prayer is never wasted. **We cannot kneel in prayer without benefit to ourselves.** George Meredith wrote: "Those who rise from prayer better people, their prayers are answered." It is impossible to pray without being bettered; therefore all prayer is answered. The prayer itself *is* our answer.

A. Philip Parham
Letting God

Enlightenment

■ **Let us cast off deeds of darkness and put on the armor of light.** Romans 13:12

Deeds of darkness suggest secrecy, shame and fear, the chains of sin, the power of evil; they are what we reject every time we remember our baptismal promises; they represent all we must let go if we are to progress in our journey—not only destructive patterns of behavior, but crippling attitudes and unhealthy attachments.

St. Paul urges us not simply to "let go" but also to "put on." The darkness of the shroud must be replaced by the mantle of Christ's light. It is not enough to purge ourselves of darkness and to be people of the twilight; rather, we need to be bearers of light, revealers of light, so transparent with goodness that we are images of God's beauty to those around us. "Come, let us walk in the light of the Lord!" cries Isaiah. Come! **Let us be light!** Let us shine in the season of preparation for the birth of God's Light.

Elizabeth-Anne Vanek

Be people of the light
—not just people of the twilight!

A Parable Of Life

■ **God's glory will be shelter and protection . . . refuge and cover from storm and rain.** Isaiah 4:6

There once was a very poor neighborhood where the winter was very harsh. The pastor there tried to encourage people by reminding them that winter did not last forever and that soon spring would arrive and then summer and that life would be good again. But some began to criticize the pastor, claiming that reminding people about the future distracted them from present reality and their struggles to improve it.

The pastor responded: "The summer that is coming is just as real as the winter and its problems. When we speak of what is real that is never a distraction, but rather it gives the people hope. The people have the right to include the coming summer in their harsh reality, to include it in their struggles and their efforts, for summer is just as real as winter. Not to speak of summer would be a disservice, for then the people would not be considering their reality as a whole, with the hope that is part of it. Just because people are waiting for summer does not mean that they stop trying to overcome the problems of winter and make it more bearable and human."

Fr. Segundo Galilea
The Music of God

Giving Generously

■ **You received without charge, give without charge.**
Matthew 10:8

At the beginning of his public ministry, Jesus faced the question similiar to the one each of us faces: shall I use my gifts solely to advance my own ease, security and power? The disciples faced that same question. Here they were not only witnessing the healing and teaching power of Jesus, but being empowered to share in it. Heady stuff, and filled with temptations. Jesus reminds them of the source of these new gifts and instructs them to give freely what has been freely given to them.

We, too, hear the commission of Jesus to share our gifts in generous, other-centered ways. But also we feel the pull toward using our gifts to heal ourselves from further pain. Jesus reminds us that all we are and have has been given to us by a loving God who imposed no eligibility requirements in the giving. Recognizing God as the source of our gifts and the true healer of our brokenness will open our hearts to the free giving of ourselves to which Jesus calls us.

Sharon T. Santia

Jesus, help me to be generous in all things and with everyone.

Taking Comfort

■ **Comfort, give comfort to my people . . . Fear not to cry out and say to the cities of Judah, "Here is your God! Here comes with power the Lord God."**

Isaiah 40:1,9-10

You often hear well-meaning people try to give comfort to others when they have a loved one in a hospital emergency room by saying, "Where there is life, there is hope." Still, that banal-sounding phrase contains a profound truth.

Our world seems in critical condition, near death because of wars, social injustice, prejudice, pollution. Everything we do seems little better than emergency treatment, and that is small comfort. But the world is not dead. Most importantly, a surgeon, a divine physician, is even now working to repair the serious injuries. From time to time that divine physician wants us to hear, "Comfort, give comfort to my people." All will yet be well. We can do more than just wait. Hope does not mean passivity . . . but let us realize that the hope we have is derived not from human activity, however important, but from God. To all the prophets of doom we should not fear to counter with the words of hope and consolation, "Here is your God! Here comes with power the Lord God."

Fr. Charles E. Miller, C.M.
Opening the Treasures

Preparing The Way

■ **Make ready the way of the Lord; clear him a straight path.** Mark 1:3

Advent is the season of the pilgrim God, the God who hungers for our love, the God who intrudes into human history by being born as one of us. We often speak of our journey toward God, but, in reality, it is God who does most of the travelling. The God who is already present in the very depths of who we are draws nearer and invites us to respond. This God insists on breaking through the wasteland into the wilderness of our hearts.

This Advent, let us make God's path smooth. Let us remove all stones and boulders, fill in potholes and treacherous pits. Let us tear down all obstacles that stand in the way, especially the overhanging branches and piles of debris from crumbling walls. And then, when this is done, let us wait, quietly and peacefully, for the One who is to come.

Elizabeth-Anne Vanek

The Mary Jesus Loved

■ **Rejoice, O highly favored daughter! The Lord is with you. Blessed are you among women.** Luke 1:28

Meditation on what we know about the Mother of Jesus teaches us that it is only through faith that we can stay close to Jesus. Mary's faith of steel enabled her to do exactly what she had to do to be loved by her Son. She accepted his mysterious ways, she kept silent; when she did speak it was briefly and effectively . . .

The Mary of the Gospel, and not the Mary of our daydreams, is this strong woman who goes forward with robust faith, in silence, with sound judgment, and in wisdom. She is the woman who grows in her capacity to remain close to Jesus against all odds.Mary was Jesus' most perfect follower. That is why he loved her. Real devotion to Mary is devotion to the Mary Jesus loved.

Those who sidestep the Gospel in their search for Mary invent a worried mother who wants to protect her children against life. Those who seek her with the Gospel discover that she was never fearful for herself or for Jesus. She won't be fearful for us either. We must ask only one thing of her: to help us to know Jesus better and to become other Jesuses. That is asking her to be the Mary of the Gospel.

Fr. André Sève, A.A.
My Life With Jesus

Divine Depenwdence

■ **The King . . . is in your midst.** Zephaniah 3:15

During this season we often focus on the holy infant in the manger. Innocent. Appealing. Dependent. Much like babies everywhere, except that this baby is our redeemer. Unwittingly, Jesus has already begun to teach, for his dependency exemplifies a basic truth of Christianity—our dependency on God.

Having been conditioned by society to value self-sufficiency, we shun dependency. Yet we must recognize that our sovereign God controls every facet of our lives—decision-making, relationships and events. Too often we acknowledge Jesus at a distance rather than Jesus working in our lives. Our independence gets in the way.

If we are people of prayer, God will show us, through life experiences, how dependent we are in the spiritual sense. And we will be given the courage to completely surrender our wills to the divine will, which rules, not only us, but the entire universe.

Virginia Ulrich

O God, help me to the see how I am dependent on you.

Living By The Holy Spirit

■ **It is by the Holy Spirit that she has conceived this child. She is to have a son and you are to name him Jesus because he will save his people from their sins.**

Matthew 1:20-21

The hidden God . . . whom we cannot see, adequately define or clearly explain has indeed revealed the divine person. But God has not manifested in clear light the inner mystery of the hidden divine nature. What God has revealed in the Gospel is the divine love for human beings. This love has opened to us a way of salvation, in which we hear God's voice calling us to a fulfillment which we do not at first understand, but which can be attained if we obey God's mysterious will. This will is something more than external law. **It is a life in which God lives in us through the Holy Spirit.**

Christianity is first of all a way of life rather than a way of thought. Merely to study Christian truths and gain intellectual understanding of them is not enough. Indeed, study does not, by itself, bring us to a complete understanding of them. It is only by living the Christian life that we come to understand the full meaning of the Christian message.

Thomas Merton
"Honorable Reader"

Gifts Of Gold

■ **The Lord . . . will purify the sons of Levi, refining them like gold or like silver that they may offer due sacrifice.** Malachi 3:3

How good it is to desire to be pure, unalloyed gold, no atoms of us withheld from God and reserved for egotistical purposes or for idols. To make this desire a reality, we should not fear to be tested by fire. We can accept the pains of misunderstanding, persecution, physical or mental illness, the suffering of loved ones, all as somehow essential to our ultimate formation in the furnace of God's love . . .

Gold is the most malleable and ductile of metals. Yielding easily to the artist's touch, it is made useful and beautiful. Would that we were as docile in the hands of the Master Artist. If every day we would heed God's voice urging us to pursue the good, if we would be open to the human instruments God uses to shape us, and if we would respond with trust and with hope to the events God allows to happen to us, then, in Mother Teresa's words, we would truly make our lives something beautiful for God.

Sr. Mary Kathleen Glavich, S.N.D.
Voices: Messages in Gospel Symbols

Too Many Burdens

■ **For my yoke is easy and my burden light.**
Matthew 11:30

To live the Christian life, day in and day out, often seems so hard. The struggle to be faithful, to grow in holiness, to advance in giving and forgiving, can indeed be a heavy task. The good news that Jesus' yoke is easy and his burden light appears almost absurd. We don't take our Christian vocation lightly, nor do we always find it easy!

Could it be that, in the name of faith, we have taken on yokes and burdens that were never meant for us? Do we follow a "God" who has insatiable and unrealistic standards of holiness, judges without mercy, is out of touch with human fears, limitations and needs? Are we caught up in the endless dilemma of wanting to do everything, do it right and do it all the time? Are we trying to *earn* salvation, just in case God's grace isn't enough? No wonder we are weary!

The Lord of Good News invites us to lay down these self-made yokes and anxiety-ridden burdens. "Come to me," he says, "and I will give you rest."

Nancy F. Summers

Lord, help me to see which burdens to pick up and which to unload.

Gaining Strength

■ They that hope in the Lord will renew their strength, they will soar as with eagles' wings; They will run and not grow weary, walk and not grow faint.

Isaiah 40:31

Who has not witnessed or at least heard of the courage of a person with a debilitating disease or handicap? Persons of vision, seeing their plans meet opposition and hostility, continue despite the obstacles. Families, burdened with financial problems, loss of job, alcoholism or drugs, have overcome the odds. The small, the weak, the poor, the homeless and rejected; even they have stories of triumph.

Too good to be true? No. At times the truth may be more than we can bear. If we believed, we would have to claim the strength that is ours. **Being so strong may be more frightening than being weak.** When we are weak the excuses come more easily.

Sr. Ancilla Keinberger, O.P.

Come to me, all you who are weary-and find life burdensome, and I will refresh you. Matthew 11:28

Lessons In Compassion

■ **I, the Lord, your God, teach you what is for your good, and lead you on the way you should go.**

Isaiah 48:17

When things go inexplicably and drastically wrong in my life, I quarrel with this passage. But in my years of quarreling, I have made a wonderful discovery: God stays with me in the anguish of sickness or suffering and teaches me something invaluable as I move through the experience. In the rare moments when I can give God the lead as pain and confusion surround me, I find myself able to make the necessary decisions and to face harsh realities.

I am even now arguing with God over the arthritis that is forcing me to exercise more regularly, eat more nutritionally and rest more often. As God teaches me to listen to the needs of my body, I find I am learning to listen to people better, particularly those who live with considerable physical pain. Though we'll surely argue, I'm counting on God to teach me an even greater lesson—how compassion can counteract hasty judgment of others and of myself.

Sr. Audrey Synnott, R.S.M.

Gracious God, help me to accept and fully appreciate the ways you teach me compassion.

Waiting In Hope

■ **For through the Spirit, by faith, we await the hope of righteousness.** Galatians 5:5

Most of us think of waiting as something very passive, a hopeless state determined by events totally out of our hands. The bus is late? You cannot do anything about it, so you have to sit there and just wait. It is not difficult to understand the irritation people feel when somebody says, "Just wait."

But there is none of this passivity in Scripture. Those who are waiting are waiting very actively. They know that what they are waiting for is growing from the ground on which they are standing. That's the secret. The secret of waiting is the faith that the seed has been planted, that something has begun. Active waiting means to be present fully to the moment, in the conviction that something is happening where you are and that you want to be present to it. A waiting person is someone who is present to the moment, who believes that this moment is ***the moment.***

Fr. Henri J.M. Nouwen
Seeds of Hope

Our Call To Greatness

■ **May the God of peace make you perfect in holiness. May you be preserved whole and entire, spirit, soul and body; irreproachable at the coming of our Lord Jesus Christ.** 1 Thessalonians 5:23

The capital sin normally translated "sloth" is actually a kind of sadness—a sadness in view of the divine good in humanity. This sadness because of the God-given ennobling of human nature causes inactivity, depression, discouragement. But the opposite of "sloth" is magnanimity and that joy which is the fruit of the supernatural love of God . . . "Sloth" is understood to mean that "sorrow according to the world" of which St. Paul speaks . . . a lack of magnanimity and courage for the great things that are proper to the nature of the Christian. It is a kind of anxious vertigo that befalls the humans when they become aware of the height to which God has raised them. **Those trapped in "sloth" have neither the courage nor the will to be as great as they really are.** They would prefer to be less great in order thus to avoid the obligation of greatness.

Josef Pieper
On Hope

Anxiety Over Afflictions

■ **He shall rescue the afflicted when they have no one to help them.** Psalm 72:12

Some people feel guilty about their anxieties and regard them as a defect of faith. I don't agree at all. They are afflictions, not sins. Like all afflictions, they are, if we can so take them, our share in the passion of Christ . . .

In Gethsemane, it appears that the certain knowledge of his passion and death was withdrawn from Jesus . . . Lest any trial of humanity should be lacking, the torments of hope—of suspense, anxiety—were at the last moment loosed on him—the supposed possibility that, after all, he might, he just conceivably might, be spared the supreme horror . . .

We all try to accept with some sort of submission our afflictions when they actually arrive. But the prayer in Gethsemane shows that the preceding anxiety is equally God's will and equally part of our destiny. The perfect Man experienced it. And the servant is no greater than the master.

C.S. Lewis
The Joyful Christian

Jesus, help me to accept my afflictions as well as the anxiety associated with them.

Words To The Wise

■ **Blessed is she who trusted that the Lord's words to her would be fulfilled.** Luke 1:45

Christmas approaches. The time of birth is near. The season of waiting is almost over. As we begin the final week of Advent, we can prepare ourselves by asking what words the Lord has spoken to us. Have we heard the scriptural proclamation of peace and joy and made it our own? Do we believe that the birth of 2,000 years ago holds promise for those of this era, for ourselves specifically? And if we have heard and if we have believed, what difference does this make to us?

Mary heard, trusted and found blessing. God spoke the impossible and she accepted, becoming in that instant the dwelling place of the Most High. In her, the Word was fulfilled; through her, the Word became flesh. We, too, need to listen in the stillness of our hearts to the words God whispers in our waking and dreaming. We, too, need to listen to that voice close as our own thoughts, constant as the rhythm of our blood. When will we hear?

Elizabeth-Anne Vanek

Mary, help me to listen attentively and take to heart the words God speaks to me.

Leaps And Bounds

■ **Hark! my lover . . . springing across the mountains, leaping across the hills . . . gazing through the windows, peering through the lattices.** Sg. of Songs 2:8-9

Love leaps and springs. Love gazes and peers. Love watches. Love calls and invites. Love hastens. Love hastens to pour itself out lavishly. Love does not withhold the gift of itself.

Perhaps that is why we see Mary hastening across the desert hills, like the lover in the Song of Songs. She is bounding over the rugged Judean hills to greet Elizabeth. Life greeting life! When Mary enters Elizabeth's and Zechariah's house, Elizabeth knows instantly that Christmas has come.

Is that the way it is with us frail and glorious human beings? Does Christmas come every time we refuse to withhold our love? This is not a season for withholding but for outpouring. The love that must be poured out will not be found at the department stores or borrowed from a neighbor's house. That love that must be poured out lingers ever so shyly in the depths of your heart. This is the season to put away shyness and go bounding over the hills.

Sr. Macrina Wiederkehr, O.S.B.

The Courage Of Joseph

■ **Suddenly the angel of the Lord appeared in a dream and said to him, "Joseph, Son of David do not fear . . . It is by the Holy Spirit that she has conceived this child."** Matthew 1:20

Amidst the holy joy of the Christmas story, the holy sorrow and incredible courage of Joseph is often lost. Perhaps Joseph is the saint for those of us who can't quite find the Christmas spirit. How good that the God of dreams, in the form of an angel, came to calm his heavy heart. Joseph's dream angel is one of the Christmas angels.

After Joseph's dream, he was able to welcome Mary (and Jesus) into his home. Each of us would do well to pray for an Advent angel to guide us into the deepest meaning of Christmas. Then, like Joseph, we would discover in our hearts a welcome home for Jesus, for Mary and for Christmas.

Today is a day for walking with Joseph through the desert of confusion into the fields of faith.

Sr. Macrina Wiederkehr, O.S.B.

Turning Point

■ **For see the winter is past, the rains have come and gone.** Song of Songs 2:11

The winter solstice in the northern hemisphere is the halfway point in the tunnel of dark, long nights that begins in the autumn. On this short, dreary day marking the beginning of winter, we can at least look forward to spring. However dark and short the day, we are coming out of the tunnel. Spring will come.

In our daily lives, though, we don't have the same assurance that we have reached a low point and that brightness and "spring" are ahead. Sometimes we spend years in the tunnel. But our liturgy reminds us that on the very darkest day, "winter is past." Not that it will be past, but that "spring" is already here: hope came to humankind centuries ago with the birth we are soon to commemorate.

That is the message of the gospel. Even though the sorrows and difficulties of our life may be impenetrable to us, we can still be filled with hope. We are in the hands of God Omnipotent who has woven the tapestry of our lives. Our deepest, darkest winter will forever have a flicker of hope. Accept it, believe it and the flame will become a torch of trust to light our days.

Joan Zrilich

Hopes And Wishes

■ **My spirit finds joy in God my savior, for he has looked upon his servant in her lowliness.** Luke 1:47-48

Open-ended waiting such as we see in Mary is hard for us because we tend to wait for something very concrete, for something that we wish to have. Much of our waiting is full of wishes. . . and we seek to control the future. We want the future to go in a specific way, and if it does no, we are disappointed and can even slip into despair. That's why we have such a hard time waiting.

But Zechariah, Elizabeth and Mary were not filled with wishes. They were willed with hope. Hope is something very different. **Hope is trusting that something will be fulfilled, but fulfilled according to the promises and not just according to our wishes.** So hope is always open-ended. I have found it very important in my own life to let go of my wishes and start hoping. It is only when I was willing to let go of wishes that something really new, something beyond my own expectations, could happen to me.

Fr. Henri J.M. Nouwen
Seeds of Hope

Saying "Yes" As Mary Did

■ **Then Mary said: "My being proclaims the greatness of the Lord, my spirit finds joy in God my Savior."** Luke 1:46-47

Mary's gift of Jesus was a surprise. She hadn't planned for him in her life, which, until the angel's electrifying invitation, had been pretty ordinary. Her wonder and joy at this unexpected gift knew no bounds. Her appreciation for the majestic power and intimate care of God was heightened. From this moment, the way she would look at her life was changed forever.

Accepting this wonderful gift with whatever doubts or questions she might have had, Mary allowed God to be the giver without conditions. God was free to delight Mary, to cause her confusion, much thought and even pain, all through the gift of Jesus. Because of Mary's acceptance of that gift, human history was changed forever.

I, too, am asked to accept the gift of Jesus. How shall I respond today? How will my life be changed? How will others be helped through my decison?

Jean Royer

Dear God, through the example of Mary, help us to put aside our doubts and find a place for the life of your Son within us.

Words Of Christmas

■ **The virgin shall be with child, and give birth to a son, and they shall call him Emmanuel, a name which means "God with us."** Matthew 1:23

The last word on human beings is that they are loved and that they are free and able to go forward to better things, to begin all over again with the Child Jesus, to become like little children, to recover their experience of life and take up again the rebuilding of society.

This last word of hope lies behind all the good wishes we exchange and is the truth of all the gifts we give each other. Even beneath our irritability, our quarrels, our inability to get organized during the days of Christmas, beneath the divisions which sometimes happen over little things, there is the immense desire to communicate, to love, to be understood and to be loved. The Child coming among us is the sign that God has opened the door to this life-giving journey.

Cardinal Carlo Maria Martini, S.J.
Journeying with the Lord

Jesus, may I remember with deep gratitude all the glorious gifts of love this Christmas.

The Birth Of Jesus Christ

Now there were shepherds in that region living in the fields and keeping the night watch over their flock. The angel of the Lord appeared to them and the glory of the Lord shone around them, and they were struck with great fear. The angel said to them, "Do not be afraid; for behold,I proclaim to you good news of great joy that will be for all the people. For today in the city of David a savior has been born for you who is Messiah and Lord. And this will be a sign for you: you will find an infant wrapped in swaddling clothes and lying in a manger. And suddenly there was a mulitude of the heavenly host with the angel, praising God and saying, "Glory to God in the highest and on earth peace to those on whom his favor rests."

Luke 2:8-14

The Birthday Of Life

■ **The shepherds returned glorifying and praising God for all they had heard and seen.** Luke 2:20

Today our Savior is born; let us rejoice. Sadness should have no place on the birthday of life. The fear of death has been swallowed up; life brings us joy with the promise of eternal happiness. No one is shut out from this joy; all share the same reason for rejoicing.

In the fullness of time, chosen in the unfathomable depths of God's wisdom, the Son of God took for himself our common humanity in order to reconcile it with its creator . . . Let us throw off our old nature and all its ways and, as we have come to birth in Christ, let us renounce the works of the flesh.

Christian, remember your dignity, and now that you share in God's own nature, do not return by sin to your former base condition. Bear in mind who is your head and of whose body you are a member. Do not forget that you have been rescued from the power of darkness and brought into the light of God's kingdom.

St. Leo the Great

The Hands Of Jesus

■ **He, the Dayspring, shall visit us in his mercy to shine on those who sit in darkness and death's shadow, to guide our feet into the path of peace.**

Luke 1:78-79

People live in darkness all around us—the darkness and despair of those addicted to drugs and alcohol, of women and children who are victims of violence, of those imprisoned and tortured, of the poor who watch their children die. Millions are alone, hungry, and homeless while many of us celebrate Christmas securely.

How is Jesus to be born for the suffering ones? How is he light for their darkness? Perhaps through us. I remember clearly a quotation from one of my high school religion teachers that served as the basis for Catholic social action: "I have no hands but yours." We are the hands by which Jesus touches the lives of the poor, the persecuted, those in despair.

The stable of Jesus' birth reminds us that he is a very different kind of king—one born in poverty, one who comes to serve and not to be served. This Messiah we are called to follow— to serve others, be light for others. We take comfort and courage in the belief that Jesus is "Emmanuel"—"God with us" —to guide our feet into the path of peace.

James McGinnis

No Lasting Home Here

■ **All the religions of the world believe in a divinity. But not all believe in a future life. The sign of a true believer is not only to believe in God, but in a God who offers us everlasting life. What changes our attitude toward life is not so much belief in God, but rather the conviction that our definitive dwelling is not here.**

Father Segundo Galilea

Have no love for the world,
nor the things that the world affords.
If anyone loves the world,
the Father's love has no place in that one
for nothing that the world affords comes from
the Father. Carnal allurements,
enticements for the eye,
the life of empty show—
all these are from the world.
And the world with its seductions is passing away
but the one who does God's will
endures forever.

1 John 2:15-17

Innocent Victims

■ **He ordered the massacre of all the boys two years old and under.** Matthew 2:16

Hearts easily warm to innocent children who need our protection. But what of others—the poor, the elderly, the sick, the mentally handicapped. Sometimes "innocents" come wrapped in smelly clothes or look from confused and glazed eyes at a world they don't understand.

These innocent victims of intolerance and prejudice should also cry out to our hearts and minds for justice. It is just that sometimes we would rather not hear them, not acknowledge them, not have to deal with the problems of the *anawim* ("the poor ones") among us.

If we have ever turned aside from a group of mentally handicapped children, if we instinctively avoid the areas of the homeless poor, if we aren't "comfortable" with the sick and dying, perhaps we should question our own true attitudes toward our brothers and sisters, all of our brothers and sisters.

Joan Weber Laflamme

The Poison Of Hatred

■ **The one who claims to be in the light, but hates a brother all the while, remains in darkness.** 1 John 2:9

Once there were two fiercely competitive merchants whose stores were across the street from each other. Each determined success by how much more business he had than the other. One would taunt the other when a customer made a purchase at his store.

One day God sent an angel to one of the merchants with an offer. "Whatever you desire you will receive. Ask for riches, long life, healthy children, the wish is yours. There is only one stipulation. Whatever you receive, your competitor will get twice as much. If you ask for 1000 gold coins, he will receive 2000. If you become famous, he will become twice as famous. This is God's way of teaching you a lesson."

The merchant thought for a moment. "Aha! You will give me anything I request?" As his face darkened he said, "I ask that you strike me blind in one eye."

William R. White
Stories for Telling

Time And Eternity

■ **Now, Master, you can dismiss your servant in peace; you have fulfilled your work. For my eyes have witnessed your saving deed displayed for all the people to see.** Luke 2:29-31

O Lord, you are still in the process of your coming. Your appearance in the form of a slave was only the beginning of your coming, a beginning in which you chose to redeem people by embracing the very slavery from which you were freeing them . . .

Actually you haven't come—you're still coming. From your incarnation to the end of this era is only an instant, even though millennia may elapse and, being blessed by you, pass on to become a small part of this instant. It is all only the one, single moment of your single act, which catches up our destiny into your own human life, and sweeps us along to our eternal home in the broad expanses of your divine life . . . There is only a single period left in this world: your Advent. When this last day comes to a close, then there will be no more time, but only you in your eternity.

Fr. Karl Rahner, S.J.
Encounters With Silence

Breaking Through

■ **An angel of the Lord appeared to Joseph in a dream** . . . Matthew 2:13

After a disappointment surrounding a Christmas holiday meal, I put on my radio headset and took a walk alone. It was a dreary day and the music was bittersweet—all perfect background to feel sorry for one's self, which was what I was doing more or less. After I had walked a few blocks in the gloom, some faint sound above me penetrated through my earphones. Annoyed, I took them off to see what was disrupting my melancholy. What I heard was geese honking. Then I saw faintly through the low clouds their V-shaped formation. *Why are geese still flying south over St. Louis several days* ***after*** *Christmas?* Then my heart lurched in an overwhelming feeling of praise to God and gratitude for these tardy geese, whose message to me was: God is always trying to break through to us, out of the clouds, out of the gloom, out of bitter disappointments, at the beginning of the year and at its end, despite the earphones we put on to drown out our sorrows, despite everything we do to run from God, in dreams, at midnight, at dawn, in daylight, everywhere and always, God never stops trying to break through. Praise God!

James E. Adams

A Morning Prayer

O God, help me this day to be a ray of sunshine in all I do and say. Let me realize that I do this best by being honest and true to myself. When I pray today, help me speak from my heart and not from phony expectations. As I meet others today, help me to show the joy that is, deep down, the real me. When I work, help me to be thankful for all your gifts. When I play, may I win—if not, may it be a satisfying loss. And let me never forget today that you are with me. Amen.

James E. Adams

An Evening Prayer

Slow me down, Lord, now that it is evening. Allow my overloaded brain to stop thinking of things I didn't accomplish today and of things that need to be done tomorrow. Help me feel your calming presence. Forgive my harmful actions today, and help me to do better tomorrow. Amen.

Jean Royer

Prayer for Courage

Jesus, no fewer than fifty-four times do the Gospels record you as saying, "Do not be afraid." Yet I am afraid so often. My many fears keep me from loving and from doing your will. Increase my faith and trust in you. Help me let go of my fears one by one, dropping them like useless baggage. For it is in conquering my fears that I will become free to share fully in your divine life. Amen.

Charlotte Rancilio

Acknowledgments and Permissions

Bible quotations are from **The New American Bible**, © 1970 by the Confraternity of Christian Doctrine; **The New Revised Standard Version**, © 1989, Oxford University Press; and **Psalms Anew,** © 1986 by St. Mary's Press. Also helpful was **Bible Wisdom for Modern Living**, © 1986 by Sidgwick & Jackson, Simon and Schuster. Creative Communications for the Parish thanks those Bible publishers and the following publishers for brief excerpts from the works cited below:

A Cardinal Newman Prayerbook, compiled by Daniel M. O'Connell, Dimension Books. **A Listening Heart** by David Steindl-Rast, © 1983 by David Steindl-Rast, Crossroad Publishing. **A Tree Full of Angels** by Macrina Wiederkehr, © 1988 by Macrina Wiederkehr, Harper & Row. **An Augustine Treasury**, © 1981 by The Daughters of St. Paul, St. Paul Books. **A Vow of Conversation,** Thomas Merton, © 1988 by the Merton Legacy Trust, Farrar Straus Giroux. □ **Being in Love** by William Johnston, © 1989 by William Johnston, Harper & Row. **Bible Meditations for Everyday** by John C. Kersten, © 1986 by John C. Kersten, Catholic Book Publishing. **Biblical Meditations for Lent** by Carroll Stuhlmueller, © 1978 Paulist Press. **Blessed Are You Who Believed** by Carlo Carretto, © 1982 by Search Press, Orbis Books. **Breathing Under Water**, audiocassette tape by Richard Rohr, © 1989, St. Anthony Messenger Press. □ **Courage To Be Myself** by Carlos G. Valles, © 1989 by Carlos G. Valles, S.J., Doubleday. **Conjectures of a Guilty Bystander** by Thomas Merton, © 1966 by The Abbey of Gethsemani, Doubleday. **Crisis of Faith** by Thomas Keating, © 1979 by Cistercian Abbey of Spencer, St. Bede's Publications. □ **Daily Readings with Jean Pierre de Caussade**, © 1985 The Julian Shrine, Templegate Publishers. **Daily Reflections** by Helen Steiner Rice, © 1990 by Virginia J. Ruehlmann and the Helen Steiner Rice Foundation, Fleming H. Revell. **Daily We Follow Him** by M. Basil Pennington, © 1985 the Cistercian Abbey of Spencer, Doubleday. **Dawn Without Darkness** by Anthony Padovano, © 1982 by Anthony Padovano, Paulist Press. **Darkness in the Marketplace** by Thomas H. Green, © 1981 by Ave Maria Press. **Decision** by Mark Link, © 1988 by Mark Link, Tabor Publishing. **Draw Near To God**, Pope John Paul II, © 1987 by Servant Books. □ **Encounter with God** by Morton Kelsey, © 1987 by Morton T. Kelsey, Paulist Press. **Encounters with Silence,** Karl Rahner, © 1960 by The Newman Press, Christians Classics. **Enjoy The Lord** by John Catoir, © 1978 by John Catoir, Christopher Books. □ **From the Weaver's Loom** by Donald Hanson, © 1990 by Donald Hanson, Resurrection Press. **Grace on Crutches,** © 1986 by Walter J. Burghardt, S.J., Paulist Press. **Grains of Wheat** by Kelly B. Kelly, © 1981 by K.B.Kelly, Living Flame Press. **Gratefulness: the Heart of Prayer** by David Steindl-Rast, © 1984 by David Steindl-Rast, Paulist Press. □ **Heart of Joy,** Mother Teresa, © 1987 by Jose Luis Gonzalez-Balado, Servant Books. **Healing Wounded Emotions** by Martin H. Padovani, © 1987 Martin Padovani, Twenty-Third Publications. **"Honorable Reader"**, © 1989 by the Merton Legacy Trust, Crossroad. □ **I Am Awake** by Stephen J. Rossetti, © 1987 by Stephen J. Rossetti, Paulist Press. **I Sought and I Found** by Carlo Carretto, © 1984 by Orbis Books. **In Search of the Beyond** by Carlo Carretto, © 1976 by Orbis Books. **In Pursuit of the Great White Rabbit** by Edward Hays, © 1990 by Edward M. Hays, Forest of Peace Books. **Introduction to the Devout Life** by St. Francis de Sales, © 1966 by John Ryan, Doubleday. □ **Jesus: The Word to be Spoken,** Mother Teresa, © 1986 by Angelo Devananda Scolozzi, Servant Books. **Journeying With The Lord** by Carlo Maria Martini, © 1987 by the Society of St. Paul, Alba House. □ **Kindly Light: A Cardinal Newman Prayerbook**, Daniel O'Connell, Dimension Books. □ **Letting God** by A. Philip Parham, © 1987 by A. Philip Parham, Harper & Row. Used by permission. **Life is Worth Living** by Fulton J. Sheen, © 1954 by Mission Foundations, Doubleday. **Lifesigns** by Henri J.M. Nouwen, © 1986 by Henri J.M. Nouwen, Doubleday. **Living Prayer,** as cited in **Metropolitan Anthony Daily Readings**, Modern Spirituality Series, © 1987 by Metropolitan Anthony, Templegate Publishers.**Love: A Fruit Always in Season,** Mother Teresa, © 1987 by Ignatius Press. **Love is for Living** by Carlo Carretto, © 1976 by Darton, Longman and Todd, Orbis Books. **Love Is Stronger Than Death** by Peter Kreeft, © 1979 by Peter J. Kreeft, Harper & Row. **Lovely in Eyes Not His** by Walter J. Burghhardt, S.J., © 1988 by the New York Province of the Society of Jesus, Paulist Press. □ **Making Sense Out Of Suffering** by Peter Kreeft, © 1986 by Peter J. Kreeft, Harper & Row. **Mary Today** by M. Basil Pennington, © 1987 the Cistercian Abbey of Spencer, Doubleday. **Mastering Sadhana** by Carlos G. Valles, © 1988 by Carlos G. Valles, S.J. Used by permission of Doubleday, a division of Bantam Doubleday Dell Publishing Group, Inc. **Meditations** by Chiara Lubich, © 1986 New City Press. **Meditations on the Way of the Cross,** Mother Teresa and Brother Roger, © 1987 Community of Taize, The Pilgrim Press. **My Life For The Poor,** Mother Teresa, © 1985 by Jose Luis Gonzalez-Balado & Janet N. Playfoot, Ballantine. **My Life with Jesus** by André Séve, © 1987 New City Press. □ **No Man is an Island** by Thomas Merton, © 1955 by The Abbey of Our Lady of Gethsemani, Harcourt Brace Jovanovich. □ **On Being Human**, Fulton Sheen, © 1982 by Universal Press Syndicate, Doubleday. **On Job** by Gustavo Gutierrez, © 1989 by Gustavo Gutierrez, Orbis Books. **On Hope** by Josef Pieper, © 1986 Ignatius Press. **One Minute Wisdom,** © 1985 by Anthony de Mello, Doubleday. **150 Stories** by Jack McArdle, © 1989 Jack McArdle, Twenty-Third Publications. **Open Mind, Open Heart** by Thomas Keating, © 1986 by St. Benedict's Monastery, Amity House. **Opening the Bible** by Thomas Merton, © 1970 by the Trustees of the Merton Legacy Trust, The Liturgical Press. **Opening the Treasures** by Charles E. Miller, © 1982 by the Society of St. Paul, Alba House. **Opening to God** by Thomas H. Green, © 1977 by Ave Maria Press. □ **Praying Even When the Door Seems Closed** by John Lozano, © 1989 by John Lozano, Paulist Press. **Praying Our Goodbyes** by Joyce Rupp, © 1988 Ave Maria Press. **Prayers, Poems, Meditations: John Henry Newman,** © 1989 by A.N. Wilson, Crossroad Publishing. **Prayers and Devotions from Pope John Paul II**, Peter Canisius van Lierde, © 1984 by The K.S. Giniger Company, Regnery Gateway. **Prayers of a Plantary Pilgrim** by Edward Hays, © 1988 by Edward M. Hays, Forest of Peace Books. **Parochial and Plain Sermons** by John Newman, as cited in **The Spirituality of John Henry Newman,** © 1977 bt the Birmingham Oratory, Winston Press. □ **Questions for Living** by Dom Helder Camara, © 1987 by Orbis Books. □ **Sadhana: A Way to God** by Anthony de Mello, © 1978 by Anthony de Mello, Doubleday. **Seeds of Hope,** Henri J. M. Nouwen, edited by Robert Durback, © 1989 by Robert Durback, Bantam Books. **Seeking the Face of God** by William H. Shannon, © 1988 by William H. Shannon, Harper & Row. **Simply Sane** by Gerald May, © 1977 by Gerald May, Crossroad Publishing. **Speaking of Silence,** © 1987 by Naropa Institute, Paulist Press. **Spiritual Direction and Meditation** by Thomas Merton, © 1960 by The Order of St. Benedict, The Liturgical Press. **Stories**

for the Journey by William R. White, © 1988 Augsburg Publishing House. **Stories for Telling** by William R. White, © 1986 by Augsburg Publishing House. **Stumbling Blocks or Stepping Stones** by Benedict J. Groeschel, © 1987 by Benedict Groeschel, Paulist Press. □ **Taking Flight** by Anthony de Mello, © 1988 by the Center for Spiritual Exchange. Used by permission of Doubleday, a division of Bantam Doubleday Dell Publishing Group, Inc. **The Art of Choosing** by Carlos G. Valles, © 1989 by Carlos G. Valles, S.J., Doubleday. **The Choice to be Human** by Eugene Kennedy, © 1985 by Eugene Kennedy, Doubleday. **The God Who Comes** by Carlo Carretto, © 1974 by Orbis Books. **The Great Themes of Scripture: New Testament** , © 1988 Richard Rohr and Joseph Martos, St. Anthony Messenger Press. **The Heart of the Enlightened** by Anthony de Mello, © 1989 by the Center for Spiritual Exchange, Doubleday. **The Inn of the Samaritan** by Donald X. Burt, © 1983 by The Order of St. Benedict, Collegeville, MN, The Liturgical Press. **The Joyful Christian,** C.S. Lewis, © 1977 by Macmillian Publishing. **The Irrational Season** by Madeleine L'Engle, © 1977 by Crosswicks, Harper & Row. **The Light of Christ**, Pope John Paul II meditations, © 1981 by Tony Castle, Crossroad Publishing. **The Music of God** by Segundo Galilea, © 1988 by Meyer-Stone Books, Meyer-Stone Books. **The Patience of God** by Valentino Del Mazza, © 1985 by The Daughters of St. Paul, St. Paul Books. **The Prayers of Father Killian** by Killian Speckner, © 1986 by Father Killian Speckner, Paraclete Press. Used by permission. **The Reed of God** by Caryll Houselander, © 1944 by Caryll Houselander, Christian Classics. **The Road to Daybreak** by Henri J.M. Nouwen, © 1988 by Henri J.M. Nouwen, Doubleday. **The Road to Joy**, letters of Thomas Merton edited by Robert E. Daggy, © 1989 by the Merton Legacy Trust, Farrar Straus Giroux. **The Rush to Resurrection** by Donald X. Burt, © 1985 by The Order of St. Benedict, Collegeville, MN., The Liturgical Press.**The Secret Trees** by Luci Shaw, © 1976 by Luci Shaw, Henry Shaw Publishers. **The Sower's Seed** by Brian Cavanaugh, © 1990 by Brian Cavanaugh, TOR, Paulist Press. **The Ten Commandments** by Alfred McBride, © 1990 by Alfred McBride, St. Anthony Messenger Press. **The Wit and Wisdom of Bishop Fulton Sheen**, © 1968 by Bill Adler, Doubleday. **The Way of the Heart,** © 1981 by Henri J.M. Nouwen, Harper & Row. **Thomas Merton in Alaska**, © 1989 by the Trustees of the Merton Legacy Trust, New Directions Books. **Total Surrender**, Mother Teresa, © 1985 by Missionaries of Charity and Angelo Devananda Scolozzi, Servant Books. **Thoughts in Solitude** by Thomas Merton, © 1958 by the Abbey of Gethsemani, Farrar Straus Giroux. **Through Seasons of the Heart**, John Powell, © 1987 by Tabor Publishing. □ **Voices: Messages in Gospel Symbols** by Mary Kathleen Glavich, © 1987 by M.K. Glavich, Twenty-Third Publications. □ **Walk with Jesus: Stations of the Cross** by Henri J.M. Nouwen, © 1990 Henri Nouwen, Orbis Books. **When Life Hurts** by Andrew Greeley, © 1988 by Andrew Greeley, Thomas More Press. **Why Be Catholic?,** © 1989 by Richard Rohr & Joseph Martos, St. Anthony Messenger Press. **When You are Angry with God**, © 1987 by Pat McCloskey, Paulist Press. **Why O Lord?** by Carlo Carretto, © 1986 by Orbis Books. **Word into Silence**, © 1981 by John Main, Paulist Press. **Words of Faith** by Karl Rahner, © 1987 by Crossroad Publishing. Used by permission. □

Author Index

Author Index